"Four Mighty Ones Are in Every Man"

Philosophiae Doctores

Volumes published before

Dóra Janzer Csikós

"Four Mighty Ones Are in Every Man"

The Development of the Fourfold in Blake

AKADÉMIAI KIADÓ, BUDAPEST

ISBN 963 05 7936 7
ISSN 1587-7930

Published by Akadémiai Kiadó
P.O. Box 245, H-1519 Budapest, Hungary
www.akkrt.hu

Printed in Hungary

For my parents

CONTENTS

INTRODUCTION

O why was I born with a different face
Why was I not born like the rest of my race
When I look each one starts! when I speak I offend
Then I'm silent & passive & lose every Friend

Then my verse I dishonour. My pictures despise
My person degrade & my temper chastise
And the pen is my terror. the pencil my shame
All my Talents I bury, and Dead is my Fame

I am either too low or too highly priz'd
When Elate I am Envy'd, When Meek I'm despisd
William Blake

"After carefully weighing the matter, it is impossible to doubt that William Blake was the maddest of authors and artists, an extraordinary genius among madmen."

This short extract of the article that appeared in the *Fine Arts Quarterly Review* in 1864 (quoted in White 17) could be taken as a summary of the chequered critical history of Blake's oeuvre.

In the first chapter we shall give a brief survey of the diverse trends and tendencies of Blake reception and by doing so we pursue a twofold purpose:

1. to place our – basically psychological – approach in the context of other critical paths;
2. to show how the major prophecies – among them *The Four Zoas*, which will be our central concern – challenge common critical concensus.

Blake enjoyed a very slight reputation in his lifetime. The reason for this, as Paul Berger notes, is that "he seems, almost purposely, to have formed his system of religion and philosophy out of everything that was regarded by the 18th century as contemptible and ridiculous" (14). He was virtually unknown as a poet – the only three articles that appeared in Blake's lifetime appreciated him as a visual artist, mainly his illustrations to Blair's *The Grave* – , and except for the *Songs of Innocence* and *Songs of Experience* his contemporaries dismissed him as an eccentric little madman. "At least twenty-two copies of the single volume *Songs of Innocence* and twenty-seven of the combined *Innocence and Experience* were printed; thus, these songs were by far the most widely circulated of Blake's works. [...] Whatever literary reputation Blake had in his time, an age when Byron's first editions of 18,000 sold out overnight, rested on the *Songs*" (Johnson and Grant 15–16).

Blake's isolation as a poet may partly be attributed to his unusual mode of publication. His only volume of poems that was printed in the traditional way was the *Poetical Sketches;* everything that followed was either etched/printed or left in manuscript. The fact that Blake took pains to produce handmade editions, each of them different from the other in some respect, may be seen as an adherence to his idea of the particularity of art and a rejection to accept that genuine art can be mechanically generated mass-production.

While the *Songs* were praised for their inimitable beauty, his later mythopoeic prophecies were no longer acceptable by Augustan standards[1] and by Blake's time "the

---

[1] "The only form of mythopoeia allowed by Augustan standards is personification for that assumes the superiority of the abstract to the concrete and brings out an underlying moral antithesis in life" (Frye, *Fearful* 165). All Blake's Annotations and Marginalia prove that this form of mythopoeia was unacceptable for him.

contrapuntal symbolism of the Renaissance" – which he revived – "fell out of favor" (Frye, *Fearful* 164).

After the compilation of *The Everlasting Gospel* in 1818, Blake virtually abandoned writing and immersed in visual arts; in the prolific years between 1818 and 1827 he drew and engraved his magnificent series of illustrations to The Book of Job and to Dante. He died, in 1827, as a painter and engraver, surrounded by a number of young artists – among them John Linnell and Samuel Palmer – who looked upon him as their master. It was these young artists who passed on to Alexander Gilchrist, Charles Algernon Swinburne and William Michael Rossetti their knowledge of Blake. The period of almost total neglect (between 1827 and 1863 only three magazine articles appeared on Blake,[2] and even though his first biography by Frederick Tatham was compiled by around 1832, it was only brought out in 1906) was broken by the publication of Gilchrist's *Life of William Blake, "Pictor Ignotus"*. This biography is the platform from which Blake's twentieth-century reputation was launched. Although Gilchrist has distinct biases and at some points his accounts are even mythical, it remains an indispensable source of, and companion to, Blake's life.

More important than this, the biography led to the publication of some of Blake's works. Most of Blake's nineteenth-century editors were poets themselves (Swinburne, Rossetti and Yeats, to mention only the most outstanding names) and this – beside the obvious advantages – had its "side effects": they had their own ideas of poetry and very often "corrected" Blake's "versions" accordingly, thereby producing editions of limited reliability.[3] Yet, this first period in the reception of Blake,[4] the preservation of basic documents characterised by biographical and archival interests, "often rather private and amateur, in which Blake was treated as something between a household god and a familiar spirit" (Mitchell, *Dangerous* 410), made it possible for Blake to break out of total obscurity and cleared the way for the second phase in Blake scholarship, that of appropriation and interpretation.

While Blake's contemporaries – with a few notable exceptions – confined their understanding and approval to the early works, like the *Poetical Sketches* and the *Songs of Innocence and of Experience*,[5] and praised them for their incomparable beauty and clarity, early Blake critics took the opposite track of regarding the mysticism of his minor

---

[2] For incidental references to Blake before 1863 see: *A Blake Bibliography*, edited by Bentley and Nurmi.

[3] The first reliable editions came out in the twentieth century: Sampson (1905); Sloss and Wallis (1926).

[4] Right at the outset it should be emphasized that the four periods – later to be identified – overlap, they are diachronic as well as synchronic.

[5] In March 1811, H. Crabb Robinson showed William Hazlitt some of the *Songs of Innocence*. Hazlitt found them beautiful "only too deep for the vulgar" (Lindsay 218).

A. Cunningham in his *Lives of the Most Eminent British Painters, Sculptors and Architects* (1830) notes the following about Blake's composite art: "If we look at the man through his best and most intelligible works, we shall find that he who could produce the Songs of Innocence and of Experience, the Gates of Paradise, and the Inventions for Job, was a possessor of very lofty faculties, with no common skill in art, and moreover that, both in thought and mode of treatment, he was a decided original. But should we, shutting our eyes to the merits of those works, determine to weigh his worth by *Urizen*, his 'Prophecies of Europe and America', and his *Jerusalem*, our conclusion would be very unfavourable; we would say that, with much freedom of composition and boldness of posture, he was unmeaning, mystical, and extravagant, and that his original mode of working out his conceptions was little more than a brilliant way of animating absurdity" (quoted in White 15).

This opinion is not uncommon even today: "It is one of the miracles of nature that [Blake's] monstrously egocentric world view should have led to such incredibly fine poetry – at least in Blake's youth. (The prophetic books of his 'maturity' are another matter.)" (Moore 182).

prophecies as the greatest achievement of his poetry[6] (still reluctant to accept the later, major epics, *The Four Zoas, Milton* and *Jerusalem*[7]).

At the beginning of our century the emphasis was steadily shifting from the visual aspects of Blake's art to the verbal. As it is appropriate in that intellectual climate, the mystic Blake dominated the scene for three decades (e.g., Butterworth; Ba-Han; White). Eighty years after his death, Blake became a "fad" among certain social circles about whom the following caricature appeared in *Nation*:

> There is a class of hungry souls who, having graduated from Dante, Shelley, Whitman, and a succession of other gospels, have at last fixed their intellectual teeth on Blake. You will meet little circles of them here and there in the country, sad-eyed women, feline-looking men, who find in the *Prophetic Books* the last words of spiritual truth. (Quoted in White 20)

Although "mad Blake" survived[8], he – synchronically – was promoted to the status of the most arresting poet of English literature. "Blake's thought was of the clearest and deepest; his poetry of the subtlest and strongest; his painting of the highest and most luminous. He tried to solve problems which concern us all, and his answers to them are such as to place him among the thinkers of several centuries" (Damon, *William Blake* IX).[9]

From approximately the 1930s new approaches have emerged, and Blake the mystic has given way to Blake the philosopher, Blake the Christian prophet or to Blake the "politician". The most seminal study to appear, which, without any doubt, dominated Blake scholarship for over forty years, is Northrop Frye's *Fearful Symmetry*. Frye's account of Blake's mythological/mythical/visionary universe – though challenged at certain points – has remained an indispensable companion to novice readers and scholars alike. Relying heavily on Frye, David V. Erdman presented a completely new Blake: the social and

---

[6] "Blake is generally known for his inimitable lyrics. To the ordinary reader, his Prophetic Works are sealed with seven seals. Indeed, they suggest to him the wild outpourings of a fevered brain. Beneath all the outward confusion, there is, however, a continuous vein of clear and consistent mystical thought" (Ba-Han 4).

In 1981 Marilyn Butler formulated a similar opinion in *Romantics, Rebels, and Reactionaries*: "Most of [Blake's] best literary work" is done by 1795; afterward it "has the flavour of private world-building, of internalized religious comfort", of "an increasingly private mythology, which is less topical" (quoted in Goldsmith 153).

[7] Shapelessness and abstraction are the two most commonly cited "defects" of these epics: "For all the achievement of the prophetic books there is something about the dogmatism which underlies them which suggests an imaginative sacrifice on the part of Blake. It is the lyrical impulse in Blake with its reliance on the unresolved world of intimation and suggestion which is the essential carrier of his belief in the civilising possibilities which lie within us" (Finch 203).

In similar vein: Morton 30 and Szegedy-Maszák 39.

[8] In 1905 H. J. Norman had the following to say about Blake in the *Journal of Mental Science*: "There is a marked lack of cohesion and such an irregular sequence of ideas as are characteristic of pronounced states of excitement; while the lack of sense of proportion which allows of the juxtaposition of refined and delicate utterances and indecent and ribald expressions is almost suggestive of a morbid brain state. It is certain, therefore, that at the time when Blake wrote this curious medley [*An Island in the Moon*] he must have been in an abnormal mental condition" (quoted in Ba-Han 204).

This opinion has continued to hold fast ever since. See, for example, Schorer and Youngquist.

[9] Arthur Symons writes in a similar vein: "Thought today, wherever it is most individual, owes either force or direction to Nietzsche. . . . No one can think and escape Nietzsche; but Nietzsche has come after Blake, and will pass before Blake passes" (3).

political thinker. "In bringing him down to earth, Erdman paradoxically managed to create an even more formidable Blake ... whose poems could deliver simultaneously profound truths about poetry and equally profound reactions to local event" (Damon, *A Blake* XIV–XV). The social-historical approach was especially typical in the 1940s and 1950s (e.g., Bronowsky; Schorer), but has ever since continued to be in the centre of interest (e.g., Altizer, *History*; Rosso and Watkins; Mee; Goldsmith; Gross; Behrendt; Bidlake; James; Aers).[10]

Blake had a rich and multifarious tradition at his disposal which – to a varying extent – furnished material for his visions. A number of scholars have tried to trace back the sources of the Blake's exuberant poetry. The most influential of them seems to be Kathleen Raine whose *William Blake and Tradition* provides an exhaustive study of the poet's "esoteric" readings and ideas. Harold Bloom's Blake, on the other hand, is a Christian visionary.[11] Yet another approach to the poet's sources is that of Charu Sheel Shing's, who claims that "from his earliest volume of poetry, the *Poetical Sketches* (1769–1778), to his last important poem, 'The Everlasing Gospel' (1818), Hindu thought continues to inform and shape [Blake's] art and vision in a significant way" (175). However seminal these studies have proved in Blake scholarship, mention should be made of the danger that lies in this approach: it may give rise to the emergence of a homogeneous Blake, whether Neoplatonic[12], Christian[13] or Gnostic[14]. As W. J. T. Mitchell put it:

> Modern criticism of Blake has generally . . . [related] him to a wide variety of traditions, and has carried this effort so far that he sometimes appears destined for utter conventionality[15], a visionary whose visions were memories of old prints and book illustrations, a Romantic who was at heart a neoclassical imitator, a prophetic poet who learned his sublime Miltonic art at the feet of William Hayley. The best Blake criticism has always attempted to mediate the claims of his individual talent with tradition, and allowed the timeless, eternally synchronic Blake to overact with his diachronic, historical contrary. (*Style* 145)

A major shift in Blake scholarship came when "static" Blake gave way to a changing, less consistent one. The former notion (a notion that informs traditional Blake studies) originated with Frye's claim that "in matters of opinion Blake shows little variation .... His principles he held with bulldog tenacity all his life" (*Fearful* 13). Although today

---

[10] The most peculiar of them is Gross who compares Blake to the Italian politician, activist and theorist Antonio Gramsci.

[11] For a detailed discussion of the possible Biblical sources of Blake's vision see Tannenbaum 8–24.

[12] ". . . nearly every one of Blake's affirmations is essentially Platonic" (Raine, *Blake* 1: 102).

[13] Bloom, in refutation to Raine's exclusively Platonic readings, claims that Blake drew heavily on the Left Wing Protestant tradition and indeed "no important aspect of Blake need be traced to those wasteland of literature, the occult and the theosophic traditions" (*The Visionary* 16).

It must be noted that Bloom's ideas later changed and from the mid-1970s he integrated Freud, Gnosticism and the Kabbala into his system.

[14] Frye, on the other hand, encourages a complex approach to Blake. He asserts that "to understand Blake's thought historically, we must keep in mind an affinity between three Renaissance traditions, the imaginative approach to God through love and beauty in Italian Platonism, the doctrine of inner inspiration in the left-wing Protestants, and the theory of creative imagination of occultism" (*Fearful* 155).

[15] Consider T. S. Eliot's remark: "We have the same respect for Blake's philosophy . . . that we have for an ingenious piece of home-made furniture: we admire the man who has put it together out of the odds and ends about the house" (156).

most critics dismiss this opinion and appreciate the changes in Blake's poetry (e.g., Hume; Ostriker; Ault, *Narrative*), we may presume that a monolithically stable Blake was at one time a necessity. "Perhaps it was the need to hold a difficult subject still long enough to get a focused likeness, and, more important, the need to deny the possibility that Blake might be intellectually erratic, even insane. If so, then a consistent Blake was the required precursor of any (memorable) Blake less consistent" (Damon, *A Blake* XV).

Once – the static – Blake gained a firm footing, the second period of Blake scholarship fulfilled its mission and gave way to the next stage. The third phase of Blake criticism, which started approximately in the 1960s, "has been the professionalization of Blake studies, the disinterested, technical justification of his work, his assimilation into the canon of mainstream English literature (the line of Chaucer, Spenser, and Milton) and the demonstration that his work conforms to . . . 'formalist' aesthetic canons" (Mitchell, *Dangerous* 410).[16]

Another dramatic shift in Blake studies discernible in the past decades is the rediscovery of Blake as a graphic artist (e.g., Bindman; Essick; Butlin; Eaves, *William Blake's*); instead of Blake's paintings and engravings or Blake's poems, now it is Blake's "composite art" that seems to arrest critics. The illuminated poems – which in their original form have so far been almost inaccessible to the public – have been published[17] to replace the "either-or" of the collections of Blake poems or Blake illustrations.

And what is happening today in the "Blake industry"? The poet-painter still engages the critics' attention, as is shown in the fact that in the past twenty years well over seventy full-length monographs were published on him, together with hundreds of articles and essays which discuss his works from diverse points of view, ranging from the more

---

[16] Similar tendencies are discernible in Hungarian Blake reception. Blake is first acknowledged as a visual artist; in 1917 József Patai features his illustrations to the Book of Job in – the February issue of – *Múlt és Jövő (Past and Future)* and describes the engravings as a treasure for all time. Patai also includes 16 illustrations from the Job series into his collection of masterpieces on Biblical subjects *(A Biblia képekben)* [The Bib]), but apart from a passing note on the conceivable madness of the poet-painter-mystic, he makes no mention of Blake as a poet.

The first appreciation of Blake's poems (as well as graphic art) comes from 1928. Antal Szerb is impressively familiar with Blake scholarship (Gilchrist, Tatham, Swinburne, Yeats, Symons, Sampson, Berger, Butterworth and Keynes – to mention just a few outstanding names), and gives an insightful analysis of Blake's visions. The key to these visions, Szerb claims, is to be found in Unio Mystica (11); the Blake he portrays – in line with many a Blake scholars in the 1920s – is a mystic, a forerunner of symbolism (12). Like his contemporaries, Szerb truly appreciates the minor prophecies but finds the major prophecies chaotic. While the incomparable beauty and rhythm of the early prophecies carry even those away who understand nothing of their allegoric meaning, claims Szerb, the later, monumental books are too abstract to enjoy (8).

A breakthrough in Blake reception came in 1959. On the one hand, the publication of – a number of – Blake's works in the Hungarian language made his poems accessible to a much wider public. On the other hand, Miklós Szenczi's foreword – as well as his later essay on Blake and Imagination – was an outstanding piece of Blake scholarship; concise yet comprehensive, erudite and up-to-date; a platform for all subsequent research.

[17] The following facsimile editions have been published by Princeton University Press Princeton Fulfillment Center: 1991: *Jerusalem* and *Songs of Innocence and of Experience*; 1993: *All Religions are One*; *There is No Natural Religion*; *The Book of Thel*; *The Marriage of Heaven and Hell* and *The Visions of the Daughters of Albion*; 1994: *Milton*; *The Ghost of Abel*; *On Homers Poetry*; *On Virgil* and [The Laocoön]; 1995: *The [First] Book of Urizen*; *The Book of Ahania* and *The Book of Los*.

traditional historical and political approaches to psychological, psychoanalytical readings[18]. The revolution in literary criticism in the 1970s reinvigorated Blake scholarship. As there is still "no settled unitary opinion about Blake, still no agreement to quite *where* in the body of literature he belongs . . . this sense of an open space in Blake . . . has made his work peculiarly available, and simultaneously peculiarly resistant, to recent changes to critical awareness" (Punter, *William Blake* 3). Structuralism, deconstruction and feminist criticism soon caught on in Blake scholarship.[19] What sets modern critics apart from the classics is a distinctive tendency discernible in a great number of writings. It seems that critics now (e.g., Lindsay; Cooper; Mellor; Storch; Moore) have set out to deface the monument that was erected by previous scholars. "Everything suggests to me that we are about to rediscover the dangerous Blake, the angry, flawed, Blake the crank who knew and repeated just every bit of thought in the eighteenth century, Blake the ingrate, the sexist, the madman, the religious fanatic, the tyrannical husband, the second-rate draughtsman" (Mitchell, *Dangerous* 411). The main problem is not the fact that Blake's supreme gifts as an artist and poet have been called into question, but that a great number of these critics build their arguments on biographical rather than poetical considerations. With these exceptions, however, we may conclude that all the diverse approaches – albeit differently and to a varying extent – contribute to a better understanding of the multivocal Blake. No single reading has yet been – or indeed is ever likely to be – sufficient to account for and explicate the genuinely difficult poems.

Although my argument will be essentially psychological, in the underlyingly tropological and anagogical interpretation of the texts we shall rely on the support and use the findings of other critical approaches, be they structuralist, feminist or mythological. Assisted by the computer analyses of Nancy M. Ide, the meticulous readings of Donald Ault, the brilliant comparative studies of David Bidney and the more traditional, though no less compelling arguments of Frye and Bloom (to mention just a few), Lipót Szondi's theory of mental functioning, more precisely the personality typology based on the Szondi test, shall be used as the main framework for clarifying my understanding of Blake's notions and as a technique for exploring the psychic preoccupations in the poems.

The platform of the analysis will be *The Four Zoas,* in which Blake first elucidates his intricate system of fourfold correlations; but the scope will not be limited to this one poem. The arguments shall be preceded and supported by references to the antecedent poems – with special focus on *The Book of Urizen,* conceptual precursor to *The Four Zoas* – as well as to poems of the same period, with occassional allusions to the later epics.

Blake's Zoas, who are the repository of Blake's deepest insights into the complexities of the human psyche, shall be explored with an eye on Lipót Szondi's system of drives, which – we hope to prove – shall be auxiliary to our fuller appreciation of *The Four Zoas.* Of the Zoas, special attention shall be payed to Urizen, the ambiguity of whose character

---

[18] Of the numerous studies and articles that analyse Blake (and/or his works) from a psychological point of view, suffice it to mention only a few here: George; Webster; Singer, *The Unholy*; Birenbaum; Youngquist; Hume; Hall; Woodman; Storch; Cramer; Punter, *Blake, Trauma;* Schuchard.

[19] An extraordinary collection of essays, edited by David Punter (1996), aims at presenting writings which best represent the diverse trends in modern Blake criticism:
New historicism: David E. James; David Aers; Psychological-psychoanalytical approach: Jean H. Hagstrum; Brenda S. Webster, *Blake, Woman*; Structuralism: George Quasha; W. J. T. Mitchell, *Visible Language.*
Deconstruction: Nelson Hilton, *Blake;* David Simpson; Feminist argument: Laura Haigwood.

14

has not been left unnoted by a number of eminent Blake scholars. Even though the ultimate goal Blake set in his writings was to enter the state of Higher Innocence, in a great majority of the poems he described the miserable world of Experience. Since Urizen is traditionally regarded as the agent of the latter, it seems vital to our understanding of the oeuvre to reconsider this concept. As the common critical concensus (of Urizen as an essentially evil character) seems highly unsatisfactory we shall carefully explore his figure and attempt to prove that beside the Orc-cycle, a Urizen-cycle also exists, with all its redeeming sides. It shall be pointed out that Blake, simultaneously with, though completely independent of his German contemporaries, Kant, Schelling and Hegel, developed his central notions strikingly congruous with their ideas of the necessity of evil and suffering to the achievement of maturity – ideas which later came to be considered as central Romantic tenets. Into his unique version of Man's educational journey, Blake incorporated a displaced theodicy – or rather *psychodicy,* with psychological forces rather than a single operative theos in the background – in which evil is justified as an important part of ontological development.[20] As the role of the evil is cast to Urizen, whose primary allusion to reason is unmistakable, his incorporation into the Blakean pantheon as an indispensable character – simultaneously with the appearance of Tharmas, most commonly equated with the senses, mark out a remarkable conceptual change between *The Book of Urizen* and *The Four Zoas,* whereby the values represented by Urizen and – in a wider context – Enlightenment ideas, which were formerly rejected, have become accepted and appreciated as integral part of Blake's visionary universe. It shall be pointed out that rather than attack Enlightenment notions, Blake transvaluated and annexed them on his own terms; the development of the fourfold, which is the repository of integrity and perfection, goes hand in hand with – and indeed signals – these vital changes in Blake's visions.

---

[20] Because of Albion's sustained internal and external reference – his portrayal as Individual Giant as well as all-inclusive Universal Man – a psychohistorical approach would also be justifiable. Psychohistory, too, explains the motivations of the individuals and with this it purports to explain the course of history. In *The Four Zoas* the interconnectedness of psychology and history is beautifully – and convincingly – delineated.

CHAPTER I

THE FOUR ZOAS

There was a myth before the myth began,
Venerable and articulate and complete.
From this the poem springs: that we live in a place
That is not our own and, much more, not ourselves.

Wallace Stevens

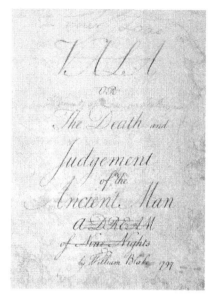

Picture 1 Vala (?1796–1807)

As we have seen in the previous chapter, the acceptance of Blake's major prophecies took a long time in coming. While the later ones, *Milton* and *Jerusalem,* have by now become accepted as part of the canon, *The Four Zoas* is still struggling to be admitted as of equal merits. The main reason, it seems, is that the epic is considered a fragment.

Having finished his minor prophecies and the watercolour drawings and engravings for an edition of Young's *Night Thoughts,* Blake started to write *Vala –* later to be revised as *The Four Zoas –* in 1797 to abandon it in 1804 for *Milton* and *Jerusalem.* Unlike the latter two, the first one was left in manuscript and was never etched, a fact that urges Frye to conclude that it was not intended to be the part of an exclusive and definitive canon. "*The Four Zoas* remains the greatest abortive masterpiece in English literature. It is not Blake's greatest poem, and by Blake's standards it is not a poem at all; but it contains some of his finest writing . . . . Anyone who cares about either poetry or painting must see in its unfinished state a major cultural disaster" (*Fearful* 269).[21]

---

[21] Unlike the majority of critics who claim that the poem is fragmentary because the Apocalypse of the final night is so abrupt that it cannot be accounted for, John Beer suggests that it is the middle sections of *The Four Zoas* that call for completion. (Personal interview with Professor John Beer, Cambridge.)

A recent critic, Andrew M. Cooper, writes in a similar – though not so appreciative a – vein: "Blake's evident abandonment of *The Four Zoas* . . . no doubt rescued the poem from the process of calcification depicted in *The Marriage of Heaven and Hell*. But of course a rescue so desperate is failure by any other name" (Cooper 56).[22] Yet, even though Blake did abandon the poem, he did not dismiss it (as the successive revisions prove) and Bentley claims that there is reason to assume that certain passages in *The Four Zoas* were borrowed from *Jerusalem,* and not the other way round (*Vala* 165).

Even those who acknowledge the greatness of the poem, attempt to retrieve the outlines of a poem – or an imagined poem – that lies behind the pages. They ignore Blake's notes *On Homers Poetry*: "Every Poem must necessarily be a perfect Unity . . . when a Work has Unity it is as much in a Part as in the Whole. the Torso is as much a Unity as the Laocoon." Rajan's distinction between incomplete and unfinished poems is especially illuminating: "Incomplete poems are poems which ought to be completed. Unfinished poems are poems which ask not to be finished, which carry within themselves the reason for arresting or effacing themselves as they do. If an unfinished poem were to be finished it would ideally erase its own significance" (Rajan 14). Unfinished as distinguished from incomplete is what the Romantics call a fragment – an authentic representation of their sense of reality, spiritual or material.[23] Peter Otto – in line with what has been said about the Romantic fragment – very convincingly suggests that there are cogent thematic and contextual reasons to surmise that when Blake finally stopped working on the manuscript of *The Four Zoas* he believed that the form it had taken was the only one that the subject matter could assume, as its form embodies the poem's insights about the nature of the fallen world and of fallen perception (144). To consider the poem unfinished rather than incomplete would help do away with at least part of the prejudice that has been accumulated ever since the birth of the poem.[24] We may conclude that the poem is unfinished in the same sense as *Kubla Khan* is – they are both organic and fully appreciable in the form they were left to us.

To claim, however, that what makes *The Four Zoas* "probably the least read of all the major English Romantic poems" (Fuller 88) is its – reputed – fragmentariness, would be a gross oversimplification, when so many incomplete/unfinished literary works have become famous and widely read (Kafka's *Das Schloß* or Camus' *Le premier homme*, to mention just a few). What, then, is the reason for the interpretative cruxes in the poem; what made the editors of the Norton Critical Edition of *Blake's Poetry and Designs* (Johnson and Grant) reduce Blake's longest poem, originally 4025 lines, to 408 lines – deeming only these intelligible, worth publishing and reception.

---

[22] Paul Mann notes that Blake's abandonment of *The Four Zoas,* usually rationalized on poetic grounds, might easily have been the result of complications in his material plan for the work: "continuing debt and the successive commercial failures of the *Night Thoughts*, and both editions of the Ballads could have . . . pushed him on toward *Milton* and *Jerusalem* and back to the techniques of illuminated printing" (*The Final* 208).

[23] For more about the Romantics' inclination towards fragments see, Péter 39.

[24] Nancy M. Ide, approaching the problem from an entirely different angle, also presents an appealing as well as compelling argument in spite of those who claim that the poem is a fragment. Her computer analysis of the images of *The Four Zoas* shows that a balanced scheme is discernible behind the narrative *(Image)*.

Before we answer the question we shall have a look at the original title of the poem: VALA / OR / The Death and Judgement of the Ancient Man / a DREAM / of Nine Nights / by William Blake 1797 (later to be retitled as *The Four Zoas: The Torments of Love & Jealousy in the Death and Judgement of Albion the Ancient Man*, in approximately 1805). Organized into nine "Nights" on the model of Young's *Night Thoughts*, the poem is Blake's first attempt to synthetize all his previous myths in a single dream; to depict the nightmare of the fall and the subsequent regeneration of Albion, the cosmic man. Paradoxically, Albion is withdrawn from the story, he is lying unconscious in a deadly sleep; the actual subject is the warfare between his four primary attitudes and their emanations. They all present the story of their fall from their own point of view, the one voice disintegrates into a plurality of voices and the result is a constantly shifting perspective.

The major challenge of reception then, we can conclude, is to be found in Blake's invention of the dream technique, which S. Foster Damon considers the poet's greatest contribution to literary methods. "This technique destroys the effect of a continuous and logical narrative. It permits the tangling of many threads, abrupt changes of the subject, recurrent repetitions, obscure cross references, sudden intrusions, even out-and-out contradictions. Crucial scenes are omitted; others are expanded out of all seeming proportion" (*A Blake* 143).

Since connective devices are muted – if provided at all – active participation and a "willing suspension of disbelief" are required of the reader to fill in the blanks in the disrupted narrative.

Besides the suppression or exclusion of elements from the narrative field, the multiplicity of voices presents additional difficulties. Since the four members of Albion – the four Zoas – and their emanations, coeternal and coexistent, are mutually interconnected in the one body of Albion, the fall of one inevitably means the fall of the others, so we would expect their individually related stories to be substantially similar and congruent. Yet, due to the different perspectives – "a series of incommensurable universes which intersect precisely at their lacunae" (Ault, *Incommensurability* 299) – and the different starting points from which the respective accounts of the fall commence,[25] these juxtaposed stories and interpolated visions not only complement one another, but also render each thematic fragment even more difficult to reconcile and synchretize. This may have caused Paul Cantor ro remark that "certainly no creation myth has ever done a better job of conveying a sense of the initial chaos out of which the world began" (quoted in Pierce 93).

To avoid total chaos, however, three basic methods are employed with the help of which the multiple styles and genres that contain multiple perspectives can hold these perspectives in dynamic tension.

---

[25] Compare, for example, Luvah's (II, 26–27:80–110) and Ahania's (III, 39–42:31–105) point of view or the account given by Enitharmon (I, 10–11:260–280) and the Spectre of Urthona (IV, 50:84–110).

1. At those points where the perspectives are difficult to accord, Blake uses overlapping imagery, diction and syntax.[26] The repetition of certain key elements in different contexts is used to communicate to the reader the significance of the given contextual variation in the overall structure.

2. The other technique typically used is what we may call, adopting Brian Wilkie's recent coinage, a *prequel* meaning a unit composed later but relating an earlier part of the story (16).[27] These prequels form "an increasingly comprehensive and progressively detailed texture of imaginatively interrelated and mutually reflecting events" (Kittel 128) allowing the scattered portions to add up to a coherent (or at least "recoverable") – though certainly taxing – narrative.

3. Blake's use of *typology* also facilitates our apprehension of the interconnected threads of actions. The significance of the use of typology is two-fold. Types provided Blake with an "intellectual shorthand" (Tannenbaum 118) that would permit an easier understanding of highly complex ideas. Secondly, typology significantly contributes to a fuller appreciation of the extratemporaneous aspect of Blake's myth. Because of its vertical view of history in which events are not related to each other chronologically but thematically, typology divorces these events "from any chronological matrix. . . . Time remains fixed and all events are perceived to be contemporaneous; past, present and future are fused through the perception of those events as repetitions of a single paradigmatic event" (Tannenbaum 118–119).

As opposed to critics who regarded Blake's new narrative technique as a stumbling block and a proof of the lost poetic control,[28] the majority of recent Blake scholars today attribute special significance to this unrewarding method and try to find the poet's

---

[26] Several critics have noted the reflections of Night I in Night IX, regarding it as an indication that Night I represents the inversion of the apocalypse in Night IX (e.g., Wilkie and Johnson 11).

The recurrent images (such as agricultural labour – harvest, plowing, sowing, wine, youth, blood, marriage feast) help us recognize the substantial interrelatedness of characters and events. Nancy M. Ide has identified 196 such image groups (*Image* 126). She points out – based on her computer analysis of *The Four Zoas*, its imagery, their density and frequency distribution – that the imagistic allusions remind the reader of the earlier scene in which they were used, but the fact that these images appear in a new context, surrounded by new images, fundamentally alters the meaning of the whole. "Thus the reader is forced to reconsider his earlier perception, and by recognizing a second perspective, moves beyond the viewpoint defined by one or the other of these perspectives and subsumes the two. . . . The appearance of images from earlier portions of the text invokes alternative connotations, and in comparing them the reader moves to a higher level of abstraction, and recognizes not only that alternative meanings exist, but also that meaning is substantially defined by context" (130).

For related matters see also: Ide, *Identifying* and *A Statistical*.

[27] A typical example for a prequel is the account of the disintegration related by the Messengers from Beulah (I, 21–22:476–550) and the Spectre of Urthona's description of the fall (VII, 84:278–95).

What Wilkie calls a prequel, Donald Ault terms as "perspective analysis": "A simple perspective analysis of a prior event re-enacts the same event within the same fictional framework – as when the initial conversation in the poem between Tharmas and Enion is twice re-enacted, once in the metaphorical action of weaving and once again in the metaphor of sexual union. . . . The most complex mode of perspective analysis 'embeds' subsequent events in prior plots. . . . An embedded plot means that previous actions are being re-enacted within a new perspective, thereby revealing information suppressed within the previous fictional framework" (*Incommensurability* 300).

[28] A recent example for this prevailing opinion: "The loose forked tongue of *The Four Zoas* is where Blake left off before beginning *Milton*; by now accepting this tongue as the only one he's got, Blake will perhaps be able to make it speak true, thus recovering poetic control. . . . The runaway tongue of *The Four Zoas* is a form of wandering erroneous and forlorn" (Cooper 64–65).

motivations for employing such a taxing narrative. Although their point of departure is substantially similar – they suppose that the verbal texture of *The Four Zoas* is functional rather than ornate – their conclusions are very different. Northrop Frye – with his customary elegance – simply states that it is difficult "because it was impossible to make [it] simpler" (quoted in Bloom, *The Visionary* 54). Morton gives a historical explanation. He contends that the poem – and indeed the other prophecies – are both grotesque and obscure because Blake was unable to relate his reality to that of everyday life. But more importantly it was a characteristic of the strange sects (whose ideas Blake seems to have found appealing) that regarded themselves as the possessors and guardians of a secret doctrine, not to be easily revealed to the uninitiated. Besides being intentionally secretive and obscure, Blake must have felt it a historical necessity to conceal these ideas since these sects were often persecuted for their dangerous tenets (33). G. J. Finch cannot accept Morton's claim that Blake was *incapable of* reconciling his reality with the world. On the contrary, he finds that the fundamental challenge of Blake's poetry is

> to our hold on what we take to be real. The reconstruction of a new self and the discovery of new modes of being involves a radical assault on accepted ways of perceiving ourselves and the world around us. Poetry is not a re-creation of secondary emotions but the disclosure of an enduring inner possibility. To see it that way is to realize the possibility in ourselves. Blake's poetry is concerned to initiate us into a world where the normal rational boundaries of accustomed perception are dissolved by the indeterminancy of untrammelled experience. Such a vision inevitably involves an undermining of formal syntax and poetic structure. (200)

Finch's argument that conventional aesthetic satisfactions might have dulled our reception and resulted in a disengagement of ideas is the most widely shared opinion (e.g., Fuller).

Even though Jerome McGann's research deals with the textual disorderliness of *The Book of Urizen,* his observations seem indispensable to our full appreciation of *The Four Zoas.* His findings are all the more applicable to the poem under discussion since *The Four Zoas* was most probably intended to be the continuation of *The [First] Book of Urizen,* as the early – later erased – title, *The Book of Vala,* shows. Even more convincing is the fact that where the two poems intersect – where borrowings from *The Book of Urizen* can be found – in Nights IV and V (Pages 56 and 57), these Nights were originally called "Fourth Book" and "Book the Fifth", thus proving that both *The [First] Book of Urizen* and its continuation, *The Four Zoas,* were a deliberate parody of the Pentateuch. This obvious allusion to the Bible allows McGann to examine Blake in the light of Alexander Geddes' "Fragment Hypothesis", according to which the Bible is a disorderly text, comprising a heterogeneous collection of various materials assembled at different times by a number of editors and reductors.[29] Just like the biblical texts do not comprise a seamless narrative, the obscure pages of Blake's Bible of Hell[30] do not locate authorial

---

[29] The shifting perspectives of the characters could well correspond to this.

[30] One of the first titles of *The Four Zoas* was "The Bible of Hell, in Nocturnal Visions collected. Vol. I. Lambeth" (on the back of a Young drawing). This is the Bible of Hell that Blake promised to give the world on Plate 24 of *The Marriage of Heaven and Hell,* and whose Genesis is *The (First) Book of Urizen.*

errors or unresolved incoherences, "the textual anomalies are structural, they are part of a deliberate effort to critique the received Bible and its traditional exegetes from the point of view of the latest research findings of the new historical philology" (McGann 324).[31] Also in the Bible Blake could find a principle of form based not on external rules but on a principle of inner coherence. "Taking individual units of history, poetry, or oratory as his working blocks, he was not bound by chronological or historical order, nor was he obliged to provide transitions between individual units. Meaning and coherence were created through the thematic juxtaposition of individual parts" (Tannenbaum 35–36). Once we accept McGann's contentions, all the formal problems discussed so far seem to be resolved, and the diagrammatic design of *The Four Zoas* becomes deliberate architecture.

As we have seen, the attempts at unravelling the textual idiosyncrasies already yielded to conceptual polemics. In the following passages the interpretative problems shall be considered; we shall endeavour to find out what it is in *The Four Zoas* that invite such a wide variety of readings.

The most enigmatic of the three major prophecies, *The Four Zoas* has been understood as the story of the Napoleonic wars and Blake's England (Bronowsky; Erdman, *Prophet*), a narrative relating Blake's marital problems (Singer, *The Unholy*), Hegel's dialectics "re-written" in poetic terms (Altizer, *The New;* Punter, *Blake, Hegel*), an attempt to write the first psychological epic (George), even as a proof of Blake's antifeminism (Mellor) and homosexuality (Storch), or the poet's argument for the necessity of representational government (Goldsmith), to give just a random selection.

The reason why the poem yields to various (extraliterary) emphases is to be found in the simultaneity of its reference. The myth of Albion is at once external and internal; the span of reference is coterminous with his life in this world, the action takes place simultaneously within the consciousness of the human race over the course of history and within the mind of the individual in his lifetime.[32] Albion is at once the Father of all Humanity ("From Albions Loins fled all Peoples and Nations of the Earth" [II, 25:43]), comprising all men in history, and an individual giant, "whose History Preceded that of the Hebrews & in whose Sleep, or Chaos, Creation began" (*VLJ* 80–81). This human unity identified with the cosmic wholeness, termed by H. N. Fairchild as *anthropopantheism* (quoted in Casier 525)[33] is best depicted in "Albion's Dance", a colour print from 1793 (also called "Glad Day"). Albion's posture is that of the "Vitruvian Man"[34], whose extended arms and legs constitute perfect geometrical forms and thus the Man represents the whole of the Microcosm.

---

[31] About Blake's conceivable familiarity with Geddes' hypotheses see Tannenbaum 13 and 292.

[32] This is what later C. G. Jung will also conclude. He asserts that our psyche is analogous with the structure of the world; whatever happens in the universe will have its parallel in the most subjective and minute element of the psyche (*Emlékek* 401).

[33] "the Eyes are the South, and the Nostrils are the East. / And the Tongue is the West, and the Ear is the North" (*J* 12:59–60).

[34] First noted by Blunt.

Picture 2 Glad Day (colour print, 1795)

Even though the name, Albion would suggest a purely English myth, and – according to Kathleen Raine – the determining national archetype of the English is the Sleeping King[35] (which indeed corresponds with the sleeping Albion), to read Blake's epic as communicating to us an exclusively English legend is to reduce the significance the poem. The myth of a primeval giant whose fall meant the creation of this world of experience has come down to us in the figure of Adam Kadmon of the Kabbala[36] but has traces in the Greek legend of Atlas". ("The giant Albion, was Patriarch of the Atlantic, he is the Atlas of the Greeks, one of those the Greeks called Titans" [*DesC* V, 42]). Albion is sick, he has sunk into a deadly sleep, and on the external level of the allegory this loss of consciousness is emblematic of the fall of mankind from the Golden world (preserved in the memory of Atlantis), the beginning of Genesis.[37] In *The Four Zoas* Blake delineates an idiosyncratic

---

[35] The most prevailing is the legend of Arthur's death-sleep in a sacred cave, where he (surrounded by his knights) awaits the time when he will return and restore just rule in his realm (Raine, *Golgonooza* 166).

[36] Northrop Frye mentions some other legends in which the concept of the tangible world as the torn-up body of a God-Man appears: the Icelandic Ymir, the Vedic hymns, in the myth of Osiris, and in the cults of Dionysius, where the tearing into pieces is called *sparagmos* (*Fearful* 287).

[37] It is important to note here that – as the poems confirm – Blake dissents from the Old Testament in refusing to believe that the creation was preceded by chaos. The following ideas, put forth in *A Vision of the Last Judgement* (page 91), will be of primary importance to our understanding of the poems:

"Many suppose that before the Creation All was Solitude & Chaos This is the most pernicious Idea that can enter the Mind as it takes away all sublimity from the Bible & Limits All Existence to Creation & to Chaos To the Time & Space fixed by the Corporeal Vegetative Eye & leaves the Man who entertains such an Idea the habitation of Unbelieving Demons Eternity Exists and All things in Eternity Independent of Creation which was an act of Mercy."

cosmology from the creation through the apocalypse to regeneration. On the internalized level of the myth, this signifies the individual's fall from the original unity to psychic disintegration and his final resurrection. "Blake is the only Romantic poet to present a united vision of apocalypse in the mind and in history" (Rosso 186).[38] This united vision, then, creates a simultaneity of reference, which we have previously identified as the main reason for the interpretative cruxes.

Yet, we cannot claim that Blake's uniqueness is to be found in this united vision. Hesiod's *Theogony* does much the same. It imaginatively transposes its historical moment onto the cosmos and – just like *The Four Zoas* – this poem, too, is "a veritable treatise in mythical language on the structure and dynamics of the human psyche" (Austin 53). The protagonists of Blake's poems, the Zoas are (on one level of interpretation) entities that make up Albion's mind: ". . . in the Brain of Man we live, & in his circling Nerves. / . . . this bright world of all our joy is in the Human Brain" (I, 11:394–395[39]). As such, they are commonly translated into their Freudian equivalents (e.g., Kermode and Hollander 72): Los as ego, Urizen as superego, Luvah-Orc as libido and Tharmas as id. Read like this, Austin's summary of the *Theogony* is an astonishingly apt description of some of the actions and characteristics of *The Four Zoas*:

> The rise of the ego; the conflict between ego and superego; the ego's fear of the libido; the dialectic of conscious and unconscious thought processes with its strategies of distortion and evasion for disguising prohibited desires; conquest by castration; male fear of female vaginal engulfment; the passive aggression of the trickster ego – such themes, issuing from profound depths in the human psyche, inform the *Theogony*, giving it a dreamlike structure, in which clarity and obfuscation lie side by side. (Austin 54)

Yet, despite the subtle similarities between Blake's and Hesiod's poems, our contention is that Blake's figures (as well as Hesiod's) are much more profound than to be describable in Freudian terms and that the figures of the Zoas communicate to us Blake's deepest insight into mental functioning.

The Zoas

As the unusual name 'Zoa' suggests, in them we are about to meet the characters that are completely of Blake's making. The ultimate source of the term is in the Revelations of St. John, chapter 4, where the Greek word 'Zoa' is translated as 'beasts': "And round about the throne *were* four and twenty seats; and upon the seats I saw four and twenty elders sitting . . . and in the midst of the throne, and round about the throne, *were* four beasts full of eyes before and behind. . . . And the four beasts had each of them six wings

---

[38] We must complement this assertion and note that Shelley, too, in *Prometheus Unbound* has managed to present this united vision.

[39] Line numbers, continuous for each Night shall be given for ease of reference to the widely used Keynes edition as well as to the Blake *Concordance* (Erdman, *A Concordance*).

about *him*" (Revelation 4:4, 4:6–8)[40]. These four Zoa (the Greek plural is used by Blake as an English singular) are the same as the four living creature in Ezekiel's vision: "Also out of the midst thereof *came* the likeness of four living creatures" (1:5). Although the word 'zoa' does not appear in the text of *The Four Zoas*, there is a direct reference to its source:

> Four Mighty Ones are in every Man; a Perfect Unity
> Cannot Exist. but from the Universal Brotherhood of Eden
> The Universal Man. To Whom be Glory Evermore Amen
>
> [*What*] are the Natures of those Living Creatures the Heavenly Father only
> [*Knoweth*] no Individual [*Knoweth nor*] Can know in all Eternity (I, 3:4–8)

Just like Ezekiel's creatures "had the likeness of a man" (1:5), Blake's Zoas together make up Albion, the archetypal Man. The function of the Zoa in Ezekiel is to be the vehicles of the divine will, which works towards the betterment of this world. This function is expressed in the textual refrain: "And they went every one straight forward: whither the spirit was to go, they went: *and* they turned not when they went." "Whithersoever the spirit was to go, they went, thither *was their* spirit to go" (1:12; 1:20). Similarly, in Blake "the Four Living Creatures mentiond in Revelations as surrounding the Throne . . . have the chief agency in removing the old heavens & the old Earth to make way for the New Heaven & the New Earth" (*VLJ* 83–84). We can conclude, then, that both Ezekiel's and Blake's Zoa/s have an essential role in the Apocalypse. As Apocalypse is a central concern in our interpretation of *The Four Zoas,* and as in religious discourse there is some vagueness about the term, a few preliminary words are needed to clarify our understanding of the concept. *Apocalypse* may be used to denote a number of things: 1. a particular text – the Book of Revelation; 2. a biblical and intertestamental genre comprising many texts; 3. the eschatological events that happen at the end of history; 4. *revelation* or *epiphany:* and internal, psychological event; 5. a sudden, large-scale destruction or catastrophe that seems incommensurable.[41] We shall primarily use the term in the 3rd and 4th meanings – which aptly account for the fundamental differences between Ezekiel's and Blake's conceptions of eschatology. According to traditional exegesis the Last Judgement takes place in some future time in history, when the damned is punished with everlasting bloody tortures:

> And the angel thrust in his sickle into the earth, and gathered the vine of the earth, and cast it into the great winepress of the wrath of God. And the winepress was trodden without the city, and blood came out of the winepress, even unto the horse bridles, by the space of a thousand *and* six hundred furlongs. (Revelation 14:19–20)

---

[40] All quotations from the Bible are from the Authorized (King James) Version.
Cf. Blake's description:
"beheld a throne & a pavement
Of precious stones. surrounded by twenty four venerable patriarchs
And these again surrounded by four Wonders of the Almighty
Incomprehensible. pervading all amidst & round about
Fourfold each in the other reflected they are named Life's in Eternity
Four Starry Universes going forward from Eternity to Eternity" (*FZ* IX, 123:279–284)
[41] For a more detailed discussion, see Goldsmith; Abrams 38–42; Frye, *The Great* 136–138.

Even though Night IX of *The Four Zoas* describes the same event (the full title of the night is Night the Ninth Being The Last Judgement) with an imagery very similar to that of the Revelation, the underlying principles are strikingly different. As the poems prove, for Blake this "panoramic apocalypse" (Frye, *The Great* 136) and the idea of a punishing God is irreconcilable with his tenet on the Forgiveness of Sins,[42] which remains his most central teaching – one which informs and gives coherence to the oeuvre; it is present in the early *The Marriage of Heaven and Hell* and is the organizing principle of the last great poem of 1818, *The Everlasting Gospel.*

Blake's Last Judgement does not happen in a suprasensible future state[43] but – ideally – in the individual's lifetime: "The Last Judgement is an Overwhelming of Bad Art & Science. Mental Things are alone Real what is Calld Corporeal Nobody Knows of its Dwelling Place it is in Fallacy & its Existence an Imposture Where is the Existence Out of Mind or Thought Where is it but in the Mind of a Fool" (*VLJ* 94). Blake, then, relocated the apocalypse into the consciousness where it could happen in the present, thereby joining to the venerable tradition of radical Inner Light hermeneutics.[44] Instead of the concern with the panoramic apocalypse, Blake shifted the focus to what Frye termed the "second or participating apocalypse" (*The Great* 137); in *The Four Zoas* the Last Judgement brings about a *change in the ontological state* of the individual and what is achieved is what Robert Jay Lifton termed "experiential transcendence" (277), a state of extraordinary psychic unity – under the chief agency of Urthona-Los the Zoas, the aberrant faculties of the mind, reinstate the mental equilibrium – through which a symbolic immortality is reached.

> The Sun has left its blackness & has found a fresher morning
> And the mild moon rejoices in the clear & cloudless night
> And Man walks forth from midst of the fires the evil is all consumd
> His eyes behold the Angelic spheres arising night & day
>
> The stars consumd like a lamp blown out & in their stead behold
> The Expanding Eyes of Man behold the depths of wondrous worlds
> . . . .
> Urthona rises from the ruinous walls
> In all his ancient strength to form the golden armour of science For intellectual
> War The war of swords departed now
> The dark Religions are departed & sweet Science reigns (IX, 138:825–830;
> 139:851–55)

The difference between the traditional Christian reading and Blake's is best seen when we compare Michaelangelo's and Blake's depiction of the Last Judgement[45]. In keeping with the Revelation, the Apocalypse for Michaelangelo is a time of terror and devastation.

---

[42] On Blake's views about forgiveness, laws and morality see Hamblen 389–391.

[43] This is the most important lesson Urizen will learn in the final night of *The Four Zoas*: The state of supreme harmony "is always present to the wise" (121:171).

[44] About the precedents to Blake's internalised millennial pattern of thinking and on psycho-historical parallelism in Christian exegesis see Abrams 334 and 46–56.

[45] Of the following account the ideas concerning Michaelangelo's Christ were adumbrated by Kathleen Raine (*Golgonooza* 1–18).

Accordingly, Christ in his painting is a godlike man, a dominating figure of wrath, arising in condemnation. Blake, who otherwise drew heavily on his revered predecessor, depicts Jesus entirely differently. His Saviour is hardly delineated, he is equal in size with the others; he is the Divine Humanity, whose central tenet is the Forgiveness of Sins. Far from being a menacing figure, he seems to communicate good news to the people around him. In *The Last Judgement* picture of the Rosenwald Collection[46] he turns to us with an embracing gesture as if to emphasize Blake's contention: "whenever any Individual Rejects Error & Embraces Truth a Last Judgement passes upon that Individual" (*VLJ* 84). The assumption that the Last Judgement is a mental process is also proved by the fact that the upper part of the Last Judgement picture of 1806 where Jesus is seated resembles a human brain. In the 1808 depiction of the scene the outlines of a human face seem to be concealed – with Jesus enthroned in the forehead or brain.

Just like in the case of the Apocalypse, where he used the biblical material just to dissent from it, Blake takes over from the Bible the idea of the interconnectedness of the Living Creatures, as is obvious from the fact that the fall of any one Zoa inevitably brings about the fall of the other three; but substantially dissents from his source by endowing them with distinct names, characteristics and roles. His Urizen, Los, Luvah and Tharmas, besides being flesh and blood characters, possess substantial divine traits themselves; they are anthropomorphic gods or theomorphic men. This double aspect of the Zoas made Kathleen Raine coin the oxymoron, "Christian politeism" (*Blake* 1: 73), to describe Blake's imaginary world.

Mythology, Psychology and the Fourfold

Although the basic shape of *The Four Zoas*' myth is suggested by the book of Ezekiel, Blake – by creating his idiosyncratic Zoas – has imposed such a complex set of overlays over the prophet's vision that the original is hardly transparent any more. With the indwelling Zoas the emphasis has been shifted from the imminant to the immanent, a fact that made a number of Blake scholars consider him as a "pioneering mental cartographer" (Bidney 101). This notion seems all the more valid as the reader is reminded immediately at the beginning of the poem that even though *The Four Zoas* opens in a world of epic superhumanity, its cosmic superstructure is to be internalized into the individual:

> Los was the fourth immortal starry one, & in the Earth
> Of a bright Universe Empery attended day & night
> Days & nights of revolving joy, Urthona was his name
> In Eden; in the Auricular Nerves of Human life
> Which is the Earth of Eden (3–4:14–18)

Having established the right context for reading the poem, Blake proceeds to write his great epic. "Epic poetry is to literate society what mythology is to preliterate society. . . . Mythology itself has been most integrally alive in Western culture and society through

---

[46] There are three known pictures of the Last Judgement: *A Vision of the Last Judgement* of 1806 (Stirling Maxwell Collection), *The Vision of the Last Judgement* of 1808 (the Egremont Collection) and *The Last Judgement* of 1809 (Rosenwald Collection).

epic poetry, and it is above all in epic poetry that new mythologies have entered our world" (Altizer, *History* 14–15). Since myth is a way of seeing the world psychically[47] and understanding a myth, therefore, requires some understanding of the human psyche,[48] once we accept *The Four Zoas* as a myth, the psychological approaches to the poem seem once more vindicated. In *The Four Zoas* Blake indeed created what Northrop Frye came to call his "archetypal myth" (*Fearful* 168), describing the fall of Albion from the original unity, the warfare of the Zoas to gain dominance[49] the creation of the cosmos and the human body, the horrors of existence in the new world – with intermittent nostalgic accounts of the primordial state – and the final integration of the Zoas.

Mythology translates [the] intuition of unity into the image of a state of aboriginal unity existing in a primordial moment. As mythology gave way to philosophy, the intuition of unity opened into the scientific search for the fundamental elements underlying all phenomena and for the element in the human organisms that corresponds with those fundamental objective elements. Philosophy and science took us far from the images of *mythical cosmogonies, in which living beings create or emanate the world.*[50] Yet modern psychology, which reveals that each of us creates a personal, subjective cosmology, has brought us closer again to myth. The ancient cosmogonies, which science discarded, have been reinstated in modern psychological theory. (Austin 55–56)

Kerrison Preston was the first critic to point out the resemblance between Blake and Jung, the presence of the archetypes in Blake's poetry, the similarities between Blake's Zoas and Jung's psychological types as well as the parallels that can be drawn between the latter's concept of anima and animus and Blake's Zoas and Emanations (quoted in Raine 1:XXVI). The recognition that the other major psychologist of the century, Sigmund Freud's hypotheses show amazing affinity with Blake's insights, was not long in waiting (Pulley). Of Freud's notions, the idea of the ego, id and superego together with the concept of the libido, as well as the theory of the Oedipal conflict caught on in Blake criticism. The best studies, however, always tried to mediate the concepts of these two psychological trends, since neither of them can be claimed to have a one-to-one correspondance with Blake's poetry. Robert D. Hume in *The Development of Blake's Psychology* distinguishes between Blake's Freudian and Jungian periods, the first being the period of the minor prophecies (1790–1795), the second of the epics. Patricia Cramer, on the other hand, discerns both Freudian and Jungian techniques used together within the same period,

---

[47] A great majority of myths are creation myths and/or cosmogonies, The myth of Albion is necessarily a cosmogony, since Albion is sick and – as Eliade, analysing the healing rituals, noted – life/health can only be restored by re-creation, by the reiteration of the cosmogonical act (123). "Every cosmogony is a psychological theory. Purporting to explain the origin and structure of the cosmos, overtly describing the gods and their functions, cosmogonies really validate cultural values, gods being values defined and embodied. All cosmologies arise as an attempt to explain the place of the individual in society and of the anomaly of the human existence in the universe, but hypotheses regarding the origin of the world and society are, at the primary level, hypotheses regarding the origin and nature of human consciousness" (Austin 54).

[48] On the interconnectedness of myth and psychology see Birenbaum. In the same vein Frye, *Fearful* 424.

[49] Five of the six possible conflicts are described in the poem; the sixth, the conflict between Luvah and Tharmas, is developed only later, in *Jerusalem*.

[50] Cf. Blake's Living Creatures and Emanations (italics mine).

within the same poem. Her contention is that Blake "presages the Freudian method of researching the cause of mental illness by recalling past personal history[51] . . . [and] the Jungian method of dream interpretation where the dream is viewed as an image of wholeness[52]; a vision of future completeness" (532).

The aforementioned critics and trends, though very different from each other, have one thing in common: for each of them it is the *characters* in Blake's poetry that can be analysed in the light of the findings of modern psychology. For some Blake scholars, on the other hand, psychology has relevance in the understanding the *poet* himself, and not his poetry. Brenda Webster, relying on Bloom's concept of the anxiety of influence, claims that the Oedipal struggle has a central role in the oeuvre because it stands for Blake's own struggle against his – literary – predecessors (*Blake's Prophetic* 7). Paul Youngquist is of the opinion that writing for Blake had a therapeutic function, because only by hammering madness into myth could he secure his health in the face of "mental aberration" (18).

Although it has by now become customary to appreciate Blake's poetry in Jungian and Freudian terms (or terms taken from modern psychology), it should not be forgotten that psychology is not a twentieth-century phenomenon, and, as his poems eloquently prove, Blake was very much interested in the psychology of his day[53], the late eighteenth-early nineteenth century – a time when art and science were not yet so distinctly divided. Of the many competing psychologies[54] that arose as an attack against eighteenth-century empiricism and its latest form, sensationalism, the "active mind" psychologies have a distinguished role in Blake's poems; a psychology which opposes the passive mind hypotheses of empiricism by assigning an active role to the human mind.[55] For Blake – similarly to other outstanding Romantic figures – the recently revived study of physiognomy proved to be a particularly attractive and influential "active mind" theory. After a marked interest in the subject in the Renaissance, the Enlightenment brought about a decline and it was only at the end of the eighteenth century that physiognomy surfaced again, thanks to John Caspar Lavater, whose works were well-known to Blake. Blake's familiarity with and attraction to physiognomy is most clearly expressed in *A Vision of the Last Judgement*:

Every Man has Eyes Nose & Mouth this Every Idiot knows but he who enters into & discriminates most minutely the Manners & Intentions the [*Expression*] Characters in all their branches is the alone Wise or Sensible Man & on this discrimination All Art is founded. I intreat then that the Spectator will attend to the Hands & Feet to the Lineaments of the Countenances they are all descriptive of Character & not a line is drawn without intention & that most discriminate & particular (82–83)

---

[51] In the case of *The Four Zoas* the prequels seem to perform this function. As the poem proceeds they relate in more and more detail the story of the fall into disintegration of each character.

[52] The intermittent accounts of the state of their original unity can be considered as the ideal towards whose fulfilment they work – just like in Jungian therapy, where the dreamer is working towards the realization of his vision.

[53] Among the books he owned and annotated we can find: Spurzheim, J. G. *Observations on the Deranged Manifestations of the Mind, or Insanity*. London, 1817 (Bentley, *William Blake's* 209).

[54] For a detailed discussion see Hall.

[55] For a detailed discussion of active and passive mind psychologies see Pléh. An adumbration of Blake and some of these hypotheses in Szenczi, *Blake tanítása* 343.

Another theory that was incorporated in the poems was animal magnetism, "the bizarre pseudoscience that played a role in its day equivalent to Freudian and Jungian psychology in our own" (Schuchard 20). Blake participated in secret meetings of *illuminés* (Sweden-borgians, Cabalists and Freemasons), where they pursued occult studies of animal magnetism, spirit communication, automatic writing and dream analysis, many elements of which are integrated in his poetry.[56] The idea of the Universal Man may come from one of these lectures from Mainaduc, who taught that "in Man is comprised in miniature, the entire vegetating system in its greatest perfection" (Schuchard 21).

"As *the* epic poet of the late eighteenth century of 'epistemic rupture', Blake is always telling us of our origin out of that 'rupture' through the various scientific versions of 'origin' (biological, cosmological, economic, linguistic, psychological) which the 'rupture' authorized" (Hilton, *Becoming* 417). In the following it is above all the psychological account in *The Four Zoas* that shall be explored. This approach is validated by the prevalence in the poem of typological events – which are repetitions within time of paradigmatic events located outside chronological time. These typological events characteristically "become analogues of spiritual or psychological events that take place in the mind of the reader, and typological fictions will therefore usually take the form of a *psychomachia*, . . . a crisis in human consciousness, whose characters and actions are personifications of particular modes of consciousness" (Tannenbaum 119–120).

Since it is the Zoas, these interconnected mental functions, who act out the polysemantic actions of Blake's psychodicy, we would like to find a psychological hypothesis that is able to enhance our apprehension of these figures.

What are those requirements that this hypothesis should meet? Ideally, it should
1. discuss the distinct entities of the mind as distinct characters;
2. posit characters that are not static but dynamically, dialectically changing;
3. regard the characters as essentially equal, among whom no hierarchy can be discerned;
4. have a fourfold structure (or eightfold, even, because of the emanations).
These points are prerequisite because

---

[56] Traces of magnetic and electric theories can be found at various places in his poetry:
I: Fuzon, on a chariot iron-wing'd
On spiked flames rose; his hot visage
Flam'd furious! sparkles his hair & beard
Shot down his wide bosom and shoulders. (*BA*, 2:1–4)
But Urizen his mighty rage let loose in the mid deep
Sparkles of Dire affliction issud round his frozen limbs (*FZ* VIII, 100:90–91)
His belief in spirit communication and automatic writing is most clearly delineated in his letters: "Thirteen years ago. I lost a brother & with his spirit I converse daily & hourly in the Spirit. & See him in my remembrance in the regions of my Imagination. I hear his advice & even now write from his Dictate", Letter to Hayley, 6 May 1800; see also letters to Butts, 25 April and 6 July 1803.
The same notion appears in the famous preface to *Jerusalem*: "I pretend not to holiness! yet pretend to love, to see, to converse with [the Spirit of Jesus] daily, as man with man, & the more to have an interest in the Friend of Sinners. . . . When this Verse was first dictated to me I consider'd a Monotonous Cadence like that used by Milton & Shakspeare & all writers of English Blank Verse, derived from the modern bondage of Rhyming; to be a necessary and indispensable part of Verse" (3, *To the Public*).

1. Blake's Zoas, besides being mental faculties, are highly distinct personalities. They are often associated with Gods (the unfallen Urizen as Apollo, Tharmas as Zeus, for example) and as such, they represent certain *types* with general characteristic traits, but – to avoid ready categorizations and to ensure a concentrated response – they are also individuals, who are allowed their full voice. Thus, to illustrate it with a somewhat exaggerated example, Blake's Luvah is at once cognate with Dionysius and – in Steven Bidlake's reading – he is Louis XVI (as his etymology "Luvah" → "lover" → "Louvre" → "Louis" shows), for whom Vala, the mythic version of Marie-Antoinette weeps in the Gardens of Vala – perhaps a reference to the Paris mob's invasion of Versailles (11).[57]

2. Blake's characters are not static, they cannot be described with any previously known name without seriously narrowing down their scope. To name Urizen Apollo would not account for his similarities to Jehovah, just as to call him Moses would exclude a lot of characteristics of his unfallen state. Therefore idiosyncratic names were created to which we bring no memories whatsoever to allow the reader to be open to the changes in the figures. But even the characters under these peculiar names are not to be thought of as monolithic; in the course of the poem Luvah-Orc (traditionally identified with the Saviour) dialectically transforms into a character, significantly similar to his opposite, Urizen. So also, Enitharmon, once a sadistic child, gradually becomes one of the chief agents of Albion's redemption. To substantiate the claim that the Zoas cannot be confined to any rigid category, we would like to draw attention to Donald Ault's article, "Blake's De-Formation of Neo-Aristotelianism" in which he meticulously follows the changes in the characters by numbering them (Los_1, Los_2, Los_3, $Urizen_1$, $Urizen_2$, $Urizen_3$, for instance) and describes their relationships, their changes into and embeddedness in one another in complicated mathematical formulations ($Los_2 = Urizen_1[Los_1]$). The Zoas are not compartmentalized forces separable from each other; they are part of a "totality which can be projected through a flexible number of figures (Zoas, emanations, spectres, shadows) which do not act within sharply delimited boundaries. . . . The Zoas are not simply representative figures: their natures have many consistent threads but also vary in relation to a total context" (Fuller 95).

3. The assumption that all the Zoas are equally important shall be proved later in the thesis; only a few points shall be adumbrated here. Since in Blake's universe of fourfold correlations Urthona-Los is Imagination and Poetry (Damon, *A Blake* 246), and since "Los was the fourth immortal starry one" (I, 3:14), a direct reference to Nebuchadnezzar's dream in Daniel 3:25 ("I see four men loose, walking in the midst of the fire, and they have no hurt; and the form of the fourth is like the Son of God"), Los is generally regarded as the most important member of the Quaternity, under whose guidance the Last Judgement takes place in Night IX. Yet, there are subtle hints that the other three Zoas are just as indispensable.

Even though it is Los who (physically) starts the Apocalypse, he gets hurt in the constant warfare and leans on Tharmas – instinct/senses (Szenczi 16) – while performing the redemptive act: "Urthona limping from his fall on Tharmas leand / In his right hand his hammer Tharmas held his Shepherds crook" (IX, 137:775–776). Knowing that Los

---

[57] For the identification of Blake's characters with historical figures see especially Erdman, *Prophet.*

is Poetry and Tharmas is Painting (Frye, *Fearful* 277–278), their /inter/dependence may have special significance in our appreciating Blake's idea about composite art.

Even though Los is "like the Son of God", it is in Luvah's robes of blood that Jesus descends: "The Lamb of God descended thro the twelve portions of Luvah / Bearing his sorrows & rec[iev]ing all his cruel wounds" (VIII, 105:323–324). Ultimately, it is the horror at Luvah's/Jesus's crucifixion that induces Los to start the Apocalypse and ruin this world of generation.

It would seem that Los and Urizen are essentially different characters, Urizen being the opposite of all the values Los stands for. He is cruel, moralising, and restrictive, to mention only a few characteristics that are most often cited to depict his character. If Los is regarded as the most important of the Zoas, Urizen is the figure that is least respected of them. But are the two really so different? The name Los could be taken as an anagram of 'Sol', which is the Latin 'Sun'. The Sun is Urizen's domain in the system of fourfold correspondances. In *The Book of Urizen* we read that "Urizen was rent from [Los's] side" (III, 6:4), they used to be one entity. In *The Four Zoas* it is the Spectre of Urthona who is rent from Los. Since the Spectre of Urthona is the fallen aspect of Los (I, 22:523–531) we can conjecture that Urizen in some way is also the fallen aspect – or at least one of the many aspects – of Los.[58]

Finally, the essential equality of the Zoas is most explicitly formulated at the beginning of *The Four Zoas*: "Four Mighty Ones are in Every Man; a Perfect Unity / Cannot Exist. but from the Universal Brotherhood of Eden" (3:4–5).

The same idea is visually depicted in the XIVth illustration in the *Illustrations of the Book of Job*, where all the four Zoas are represented as equally radiating and beautiful.[59]

4. By the time of *The Four Zoas* Blake developed his visionary universe of fourfold correlations, which appears as the repository of perfection:

> Now I a fourfold vision see
> And a fourfold vision is given to me
> Tis fourfold in my supreme delight
> And three fold in soft Beulahs night
> And twofold Always. May God us keep
> From Single vision & Newtons sleep[60]

The dualistic view is characteristic of the world of Generation and Ulro, the two inferior states in Blake's poetry. Ulro is the lowest state, it is the material world, the place of the sleepers, spiritually dead; it is the Grave itself: "We look down into Ulro we behold the Wonders of the Grave" (*FZ* VIII, 113:223). Ulro is the state of eternal pain "where the Dead wail Night & Day" (*FZ* II, 25:71). Until *Jerusalem* (12:45–13:29) Ulro seems to be identical with Generation, "the Generation of Decay & Death" (*FZ* I, 4:21). As Blake's vision turned more and more into the direction of regeneration and redemption, besides the contraries there appeared the shapes of a threefold system,

---

[58] The essential role of the Spectre of Urthona (also called the "Spectre of the Living" [VII, 84:301]) in the Regeneration of Albion shall be discussed later.
[59] For detailed description of the illustrations see Damon, *Blake's Job*.
[60] In the letter to Butts, dated 22 November 1802.

almost always bearing some sexual connotation, like in the *Visions of the Daughters of Albion*, *The Book of Urizen* or *The Book of Ahania*. This threefold state is called Beulah. The name and the idea of the region of sexual love is taken from the biblical account of Isaiah: "Thou shalt no more be termed Forsaken; neither shall thy land any more be termed Desolate: but thou shalt be called Hephzi-bah, and thy land Beulah: for the Lord delighteth in thee, and thy land shall be married" (63:4). Of all the four states Beulah is the most ambiguous. This ambiguity is mainly due to its sexual nature and Blake's ambivalent portrayal of the role of sexuality in the fall and redemption of Man, a topic which stimulated pungent debates in the past two decades.[61]

The duality of Beulah is also a result of its position. It is an intermediary between Ulro and Eternity, a land of sweet delusion and sleep:

> There is from Great Eternity a mild & pleasant rest
> Namd Beulah a Soft Moony Universe feminine lovely
> Pure mild & Gentle given in Mercy to those who sleep
> Eternally. Created by the Lamb of God around
> On all sides within & without the Universal Man
> The Daughters of Beulah follow sleepers in all their Dreams
>   Creating Spaces lest they fall into Eternal Death (*FZ* I, 5:94–100)

Beulah is – we may conclude – the state of the unconscious, which, when dwelt in too long – as in the case of Thel in *The Book of Thel* as well as Har and Heva in *Tiriel* – reduces man to an infantile imbecility or aged ignorance. When this happens, Beulah degenerates into Ulro. But Beulah can be a redemptive state inasmuch as beyond it lies Eden into which it is possible to enter through Beulah and it is over this state that the Saviour descends to awake the dreamers.[62] As Harold Bloom put it: "Beulah is the most ambiguous state. Its innocence dwells dangerously near to ignorance, its creativity is allied to destructiveness, its beauty to terror. . . . Beulah lies beyond both mortality and despair, nor can doubt be seen from it. And yet it is upon the borders of Heaven, not Heaven himself" (*The Visionary* 16).[63] In order that Heaven may be depicted the so-far tri-partite structure was complemented with a fourth dimension: "The Sexual is Threefold: the Human is Fourfold" (*M* I, 4:5). With the appearance of Tharmas in *The Four Zoas* (up until the compilation of the minor prophecies only three of the four Zoas are mentioned by the name: Luvah, Urizen and Los) the fourth dimension is introduced; the ultimate goal, Humanity – and its corresponding state, Eden – has found a proper expression. This is not to say that Tharmas himself is the ultimate redemptive power in Blake's poetry but his appearance is inevitable in the emergence of the – redemptive – fourfold unity. In his character we witness an essential change in Blake's visionary universe. Tharmas is associated with the bodily senses which were but rejected in the earlier poems – most emphatically, perhaps in "To Tirzah". This rejection was – partly – due to a disawoval of the Enlightenment and its empiricism.

---

[61] For instance George; Ackland; Mellor; Ostriker; Storch; Webster; Cramer; Haigney; Singer, *Androgyny;* Verma; Rosso and Watkins; Goldsmith.

[62] See *FZ* I, 9:222–226 and IV, 55:248–253.

[63] See also Frye, *Fearful* 389–390.

By *The Four Zoas,* however, Enlightenment ideas seem to have become accomodated into the essentially Romantic framework of the poem. This hypothesis is substantiated by the fact that the acceptance of Tharmas/senses as a mental faculty of equal merit with Los/imagination is coincidal with a spectacular revaluation of Urizen's role whereby reason becomes a prime agent of the redemption of Man.

At this point the question why the ultimate reality is depicted as fourfold presents itself. It is tempting to subscribe to David Groves's observation who – struck by Blake's frequent use of the term "fourfold" – pursued the same question:

Contemporary readers may have detected an echo of Boston's book *Human Nature, in its Fourfold State,* a popular work of theology which went through at least two dozen editions in Britain between 1720 and 1800. The first condition is a "State of Innocence, or Primitive Integrity" which exists only at birth.

This is followed by the "State of Nature, or Entire Deprivation", in which "natural man" can "do nothing but sin". In the third state "The conscience is renewed and one apparently experiences a *"mysterious union"*, a "mystical union betwixt Christ and Believers".

The last stage is entered at death, when the ungodly see "the dark side of the cloud" while the righteous perceive "the bright side of it, shining on the godly, as they are entering upon their eternal state". (142)

Although the similarities are appealing, they are by no means compelling. The poems testify that the fourfold carries in itself the notion of perfection. As we have seen, this perfection is called Humanity or Eden, which are the regenerate Man in his new ontological state. And since his resurrected body is all Imagination

The Eternal Body of Man is The IMAGINATION.
               God himself
    that is   }   JESUS we are his Members[64]
               The Divine Body

we can conclude that Blake's fourfold Man is Man-turned-into-God, and as such, it resembles Boston's third state. But even though it is not impossible to conjecture that Blake took the term "fourfold" from Boston, it should be underlined that their concepts differed substantially, since the latter's ideas are ultimately in line with the teachings of traditional prophecy, from whose tenets Blake dissented considerably, most explicitly in his prepossession with the Forgiveness of Sins – incompatible with Boston's fourth state. Another significant difference between Boston's and Blake's fourfold worlds is that while in the first the states follow a strict chronological order, in the latter they are emphatically co-existant, the individual can enter or leave them freely.

It seems that David Groves did not find a satisfactory answer to our original question: Why the appearance of the fourfold? The most palpable explanation appears to be the simple fact that of old four has been regarded as a number suggestive of totality and

---

[64] Engraved on [The Laocoön].

perfection. The four seasons, the four compass points, the four basic elements all imply integrity, and it is this integrity of the Universal Man – in whom outward experience and inward reality merge – that is expressed in the figure of Albion. The fourfold correspondances are all-encompassing, each of the Zoas is assigned his respective part of the quaternity of totality. The following chart sums up but the most important of these correlations:[65]

Eternal Name	Luvah	Urizen	Tharmas	Urthona
Emanation	Vala	Ahania	Enion	Enitharmon
Quality	Love	Reason	Instincts/senses	Imagination
Sense	Nostrils	Eyes	Tongue	Ears
Art	Music	Architecture	Painting	Poetry
Activity	Weaver	Plowman	Shepherd	Blacksmith
Point	East	South	West	North
Element	Fire	Air	Water	Earth
Metal	Silver	Gold	Brass	Iron

Of the numerous fourfold hypotheses[66] two may have had special significance in Blake's poetry: Platonism and the Bible, both of which have been exhaustively studied by Kathleen Raine *(Blake and Tradition)* and Leslie Tannenbaum *(Biblical Tradition in Blake's Early Prophecies)* respectively.[67]

Freud and Jung

We have stated earlier that we presume that a framework that satisfies the above-discussed four points may contribute to a better understanding of Blake's figures. We shall first examine how the two psychologies that are most frequently used in Blake scholarship correspond to these expectations. (Although some of the notes on Freud's and Jung's notions might sound negative, it is important to stress that no value judgement is intended. All the statements that follow strictly explore the affinity of Freud and Jung with the prerequisites previously outlined.)

---

[65] For a more complete chart see Frye, *Fearful* 277–278 and Damon, *A Blake* 212.

[66] For a detailed description of these hypotheses see Eliade 170–185.

[67] In the Bible the quaternity or tetramorph carries a particular implication. The notion can be found in Daniel, Ezekiel and the Revelation as well as indirectly in the four evangelists and in the symbol of Christianity, the cross. But more important for us than this is what Jung noted in his *Answer to Job* where he claimed that the fourfold stands for a *more differentiated consciousness*, which characterises Man who surpassed God and became equal with Christ (72–74, 84).

In fact, as David Bidney asserts, "in *Answer to Job*, Jung depicted the whole Bible as God's incomplete search for a differentiation of consciousness that would lead to a truly satisfactory fourfold vision" (19). While Jung explores God's attempt to become Man, in Blake's poetry the opposite process is delineated: Man's endeavours to become God, or rather, (in line with Luther and Ficino) to live the God who dwells within him. Jung and Blake intersect at their notion of the fourfold.

In Freud's psychoanalytic theory the personality comprises three separate but interacting systems, the id, the ego and the superego. Although these terms seem to have taken a life of their own and very often in analytic literature they are written about as if they were a cast of characters (Aronoff et al. 462) with an existence almost independent of the person within whom they operate, they are diagrammatic; they do not impress us as real-life characters but rather as ideographs. While Blake's Zoas can be understood – using James Ogilvy's term – as *intrapersonal selves*, that is, a *plurality of selves that can exist together in one person and have different personalities,*[68] for Freud this multiplicity of individual personalities is inconceivable. As I. Sz. Kon noted, European culture and thinking tended to regard the unity and integrity of the personality as the only acceptable norm and considered the polyvalence and multiplicity of identity as pathological (64).

> Freudian psychology reflects an Enlightenment consciousness that places value in clear, unambiguous identity. . . . The value placed on unity and identity generates a suspicion of intrapersonal division. . . . Intrapersonal diffusion will be condemned as a sign of sickness. As long as unity and identity reign supreme there will be an effort to reject the notion that a personal self could be a mediation among a collection of individuated, relatively autonomous intrapersonal selves. (Ogilvy 99–100)

This rejection of the multeity-in-unity is the central crisis in *The Four Zoas*. In the poem Blake dramatises the effect of the suppression of these intrapersonal selves; the sickness of Albion is a result of the Zoas's effort to assert themselves above one another. In the spiritually healthy Man all four Zoas are present and wage their creative intellectual strife as equally important members of the human integral.

The entities in Freudian psychology are not distinct individuals and they have a relatively static set of characteristics; the id, which is completely unconscious, can never become the superego any more than the ego can become the id. The characters of Blake's myth are dialectically changing, they are changing along with the changes in the narrative.

The most conspicuous difference between Blake and Freud is that psychoanalysis is a system of tripartite structures and triadic theory. Besides the three interrelated functions, it posits three phases in the development of the personality; the oral, the anal and the genital. The Oedipus complex, which Freud considered as one of his greatest discoveries, is essentially triangular, involving the mother, the father and the child.

Although Freudian psychoanalysis does not seem to be a sufficient guide to analyse Blake's fourfold configuration, the correspondances between Blake's and Freud's threefold structures – both being essentially sexual – are striking. Diane Hume George, in her remarkable book *Blake and Freud* examines this aspect in early Blake (meaning the works until the mid 1790s) in the light of late Freud.

There is yet another point of comparison that needs to be studied. Freudian psychoanalysis is often called reductionistic because of two reasons. First, because it reduces human behaviour to the biological instincts (Aronoff et al. 466). Blake, on the other hand, is much less deterministic, in his visionary world the change in one's

---

[68] "The intrapersonal selves are best understood as different gods, that is, as different projections of different cults . . . . We each have our Dionysus, our Apollo, our Zeus and so on" (Ogilvy 103–104).

consciousness is the source of every move of the individual, and imagination – aided by the other three Zoas – is identified as the prime agent of man's actions. The integrity of imagination, reason, passion and the senses is the extra fourth fold that makes man Human in Blake's poetry. The other reason for calling Freud's psychoanalysis reductive is its past-orientedness. Its insistence on one's indebtedness to the secrets of the past, over which one has no or little control, often effects a reduction, rather than an expansion, of the identity. In Blake's formulation, which Wayne Glausser termed *expansive or Blakean psychoanalysis,* memory also plays an important role, but in a different sense.

> Although the past remains a signifying power, the patient is not enslaved to an inert set of primal conditions. The act of remembering as re-membering does not passively reproduce what has come before. It constitutes a creative judgement, happening now, in which the past and present mutually inform each other: it makes as much sense to say that the present determines the past as the past determines the present. (202)

On the poetic level, this creative participation of the Zoas in shaping their lives is made possible by the use of the prequels.

Carl Gustav Jung's analytical psychology undoubtedly shows a lot of similarities with Blake's ideas. Since Blake's Albion (at once historical-universal and individual-personal), in whose mind the actions of *The Four Zoas* take place, is asleep all through the course of the poem, we can confer that the setting of the prophecy is almost entirely in the subconscious. Jung's distinction between the two levels of the unconscious, the *personal unconscious,* which contains experiences the individual has had that were once conscious but have been forgotten or repressed, and the *collective unconscious,* which is a storehouse of memories inherited from one's ancestral past and is shared by all human beings, seem to correspond well with this double aspect of sustained internal and external reference of the Universal Man.

Jung's theory of the *archetypes* also proved to be useful in Blake scholarship (e.g., Gallant). Northrop Frye, discussing Blake's poetry in his essay, "Blake's Treatment of the Archetype", asserts that

> what finally emerged, out of one of the hottest poetic crucibles of modern times, was a poetry which consisted of almost entirely in the articulation of archetypes. By an archetype I mean an element in a work of literature, whether a character, an image, a narrative formula, or an idea, which can be assimilated to a larger unifying category. The existence of such a category depends on the existence of a unified conception of art. Blake began his prophecies with a powerfully integrated theory of the nature, structure, function, and meaning of art, and all the symbolic units of his poetry, his moods, his images, his narratives and his characters, form archetypes of that theory. (522)

Blake's poetry abound in archetypal qualities, such as youth and age, light and darkness, fire and ice, or the "Baroque imagery" of solid and liquid (Fogel 230); all these are universal images, which possess the greatest constancy and so their connotations are strikingly similar and identifiable to even novice readers of Blake. The accessibility of these archetypal images, then, serve as a counterbalance to the obscurity of the narrative, and contribute significantly to the coherence and cohesion of the loosely structured text.

Jung dissents from Freud and coincides with the ideas formulated in Blake's poems in that he believes that there is an essentially *forward-going* character to *personality development*. Man is continuously trying to realize himself, and his ultimate goal is to achieve unity within his personality. This unity is accomplished by developing all parts of his personality and not by repressing or eliminating them. Just like Blake, he insists on the validity of *spirituality* in this process (Aronoff et al. 470).

After these preliminary observations on the parallels between Blake's and Jung's notions it shall be considered how analytical psychology satisfies the four prerequisites determined earlier. Jung's system certainly corresponds to the first and fourth points. In the *Personality Types* he delineates two attitudes, introversion and extraversion, and four functions, thinking, feeling, sensing and intuiting which define eight character types altogether. Even though he describes these characters as distinct personalities (dwelling in the individual) on the basis of which we can roughly identify the four functions with the four Zoas (we cannot claim that the eight types are the Zoas and their Emanations), Urizen with thinking, Luvah with feeling, Tharmas with sensing, and Urthona-Los with intuiting,[69] there are some points which seem to render Jung's ideas incompatible with Blake's visions. Jung's types never change into one another, there appears to be no penetrability between them. Even though the personality – ideally – develops as a result of the interaction between the functions, these functions remain essentially rigid categories. Even though Jung stated that the disparate functions should be equal and none must be repressed or placed above the others, he considered it as a practically unrealizable goal. Should all four functions, Jung asserted, be developed fully, Man would become as perfect as God, which – he concluded – can never happen (*Analitikus* 126).

The divinity of man was a central tenet[70] present in almost all Blake's poems, from *The Marriage of Heaven and Hell* of 1790 ("The worship of God is. Honouring his gifts in other men each according to his genius. and loving the greatest men best, those who envy or calumniate great men hate God, for there is no other God." [22–23]) to *The Everlasting Gospel* of 1818 ("Thou art a Man God is no more / Thy own humanity learn to adore / For that is my Spirit of Life").

Another difference between the Blakean and Jungian notions seems to be in their conception of the feminine portion in man. Blake's *Emanations* have often been identified with the Jungian *anima*.[71] "According to Jung . . . an individual man changes and develops during the course of his lifetime but 'his' *anima* does not. She remains *static*, and *his only problem is to accept her existence as a portion of himself*" (Ostriker 158–159; emphasis added). The Emanations, on the other hand, are anthropomorph psychic functions, and as such are necessarily active. They are distinct personalities with individual names and identities, which they acquired after the fall. Before the fall they were the perfect counterparts of their respective Zoas, who were originally bisexual in that they contained both male and female components. In the fallen condition this unity is disrupted, the Emanations separate, and just like the Zoas, they all go through their history of

---

[69] For a Jungian interpretation of these characters see Singer, *The Unholy Bible*.

[70] "We are all coexistent with God-Members of the Divine Body-And partakers of the divine nature . . . [Jesus Christ] is the only God, ... And so am I and So are you," Blake said to Henry Crabb Robinson (Bentley, *Blake Records* 542).

[71] For instance Singer, *The Unholy Bible*; Hume; Frye, *"Blake's Treatment of the Archetype"*.

transformations and development before they can re-unite with their counterparts. Although *The Four Zoas* offers ample chances to refute the assumption that the Emanations are to be equated with the Jungian anima, suffice it to illustrate this with the example of only one of the Emanations, in whose case the progress is especially conspicuous: Enion.

Enion starts out as a jealous, cruel counterpart to Tharmas:

> I thought Tharmas a Sinner & murderd his Emanations
> His secret loves & Graces Ah me wretched What have I done
> For now I find that all those Emanations were my Childrens Souls
> And I have murderd them with Cruelty above atonement
> Those that remain have fled from my cruelty into the desarts (I, 7:163–167)

Tormented by guilt, she wanders far away to go through the experiences of fallen existence. Her introspection results in the most beautiful – and probably the most known – lament of the poem:

> What is the price of Experience do men buy it for a song
> Or wisdom for a dance in the street? No it is bought with the price
> Of all that a man hath his house his wife his children
> Wisdom is sold in the desolate market where none come to buy (II, 35:397–400)

While at first she seems to have abandoned all hope in a possible regeneration, by the end of the poem she becomes the one that foresees the coming of the Saviour and the time when the Eternal Man reassumes his ancient bliss:

> Fear not O poor forsaken one O land of briars & thorns
> Where once the Olive flourishd & the Cedar spread his wings
> Once I waild desolate like thee my fallow fields in fear
> Cried to the Churchyards & the Earthworm came in dismal state
> I found him in my bosom & I said the time of Love
> Appears upon the rocks & hills in silent shades but soon
> A voice came in the night a midnight cry upon the mountains
> Awake the bridegroom cometh I awoke to sleep no more
> . . . .
> The Lamb of God has rent the Veil of Mystery soon to return (VIII, 109:534–541; 110:556)

Enion's self-realization is then followed by her climactic re-union with Tharmas which is an inevitable step in the regeneration of Albion.

The assumption that it is difficult for the individual to accept the anima as a portion of himself, yet again sets the Jungian concept apart from Blake's Emanations. All the four Zoas are acutely aware of the existence of the female portion within them and their essential unity:

> Astonishd & Confounded [Urizen] beheld
> Her shadowy form now Separate he shudderd & was silent
> . . . .

Two wills they had two intellects & not as in times of old
This Urizen percievd & silent brooded in darkning Clouds (II, 30:203–204; 206–208)

They – consciously or not – all seek to re-establish the union with their sundered counterparts. Almost all of Tharmas's actions focus on his search for Enion, without whom he cannot live: "O fool fool to lose my sweetest bliss / Where art thou Enion ah too near to cunning too far off" (III, 45:168–169). In Blake's poem the female portion is assigned an important, active role and the interaction between male and female shapes the life of the individual.

As a conclusion we can contend that even though there are a lot of similarities between Jung's notions and the ideas formulated in Blake's poems and we shall occassionally use Jung's insights to illuminate certain passages, we should be wary of a too ready identification of their theories.

Theories of the Personality

Having studied how Freud's and Jung's theories correspond with Blake's poetic world some other theories of the personality shall be briefly referred to. Conceptions of man prior to the twentieth century were largely the works of philosophers, theologians, poets, dramatists and novelists.

The idea of the fourfold structure of the individual can be found in Plato's *Timaeus* and the fourfold scheme of the human psyche structures Hindu mythology as well as Buddhism, which also conceives of the human as the unity of three material and one spiritual entity. Though both these latter oriental traditions informed European literature and no doubt influenced Blake's vision to a great extent it is important to note that they suggest a hierarchical view[72] of the human faculties, which runs counter Blake's contention, set down immediately at the beginning of *The Four Zoas,* namely that the Brotherhood of Eden is the organic interdependence of all the four functions: "Four Mighty Ones are in every Man; a Perfect Unity / Cannot Exist. But from the Universal Brotherhood of Eden" (I, 3:4–5). The poem dramatizes the effects of the repression (or dropping out) of *any* one of these faculties.

John Beer convincingly points out the paramount influence of Jacob Boehme's ideas on Blake's universe (25–30). Boehme's fourfold hypothesis, depicted in the design entitled 'The Tree of the Soul' shows four overlapping states – the 'Dark World', corresponding to Ulro; the state of 'Fire' or 'Wrath', similar to Blake's Generation; the state of 'Light' or 'Paradise', resembling Beulah; and the supreme state, the 'Light of Majesty' reconciling all others, concurrent with Eden – coordinated by the structure of a tree.

The idea that there exist various states of the soul is of course common in Christian theology, but Boehme differs from the usual tradition at two points. Firstly, he places the 'physical' universe not, as in medieval theology, between Heaven and Hell, but beneath both of them. Secondly, he makes a separation between Heaven and Paradise

---

[72] See Sheel Shing 180.

which suggests that Paradise itself is an inferior state, not to be equated with Heaven. The latter idea falls in with Milton's cosmology, but not with those orthodox conceptions that virtually identify the two states. Blake takes over these features but differs from Boehme in one important respect; his interest is more in psychological explanation than in pietistic exhortation. (Beer 26)

The Four Zoas eloquently proves that not only did Blake think of Boehme's states as basically psychological in nature (these states being ultimately related to his system of energies, otherwise called Zoas), he dissented from the idea of the Tree of Soul inasmuch as the relationship of his Zoas cannot be aptly depicted in a vertical order which allows for only two proximal functions to be organically connected. The integrity of the Zoas may better be pictured as overlapping concentric circles, which entertain no idea of hierarchy. We cannot agree with Beer's assertion that around 1800 Blake returned to the mental universe of his youth and it gave new predominance to Boehme's paradigm so "the descending hierarchy of creative genius, human love, expressive energy and limiting reason . . . became the unchallenged order of his visionary universe" (30).

It has been suggested that for Blake the sublimity and divinity of utterance lay not in its imitation of nature but in its imitation of psychological states. Because of this psychological mimesis the Zoas – on one level of interpretation – invite psychological considerations.

It has also been pointed out that the Zoas are distinct personalities with identifyable character traits. We shall try to prove that they belong to certain psychological categories and represent different personality types.

Since ancient times there has been a great deal of speculation about types of people. The most influential personality typology comes from ancient Greece where a number of scholars, among them Aristotle, Hippocrates and Galen, elaborated the typological theory of temperament based on the conception of humours. They distinguished four such humours: blood, black bile, yellow bile and phlegm, and speculated that their combinations produce four types of temperament. They claimed that the predominance of blood resulted in a sanguine or enthusiastic temperament, the preponderance of black bile led to a melancholic disposition, the excess of yellow bile was the cause of the irascibility of the choleric type, and the apathy of the phlegmatic was due to the over-abundance of phlegm. These types are described in Lavater's *Aphorisms on Man* (1788): "Venerate four characters; the sanguine, who has checked volatility *and the rage for pleasure; the choleric, who has subdued passion and pride; the phlegmatic, emerged from indolence; and the melancholy, who has dismissed avarice, suspicion, and asperity.*"[73] Blake wrote the following marginalia to the passage: "4 most holy men". Even though the note "most holy men" could well correspond to the idea of the Living Creatures, we always have to bear in mind that the warfare of the Zoas is mental-allegorical rather than physical-biological. In one respect, however, Blake's annotation seems to be of utmost importance. He does not repudiate or privilege any one of the characters; all four of them are considered as holy. Given that the psychology of humours was conceived to be applicable to all individuals, just like to four Zoas altogether comprise the whole of mankind, our notion of Blake's conception of the Zoas as equal seems to be a tenable hypothesis.

---

[73] The agreeable passages were underlined by Blake; this is expressed by the italics.

The typology based on the humours shares the defects of all the subsequent attempts to develop a model of the personality.[74] Up until the twentieth century these models were based on the assumption that there are discreet categories of people, and the categories can be differentiated from one another by a precise list of personality characteristics. The types were qualitatively different from one another and were considered homogeneous in the sense that the people who composed a given category shared all the defining attributes. The problem with this classical conception of categories is that it is taken over from the field of logic and what is applicable to philosophy is not necessarily efficacious in psychology. In reality the categories overlap, people grade into one another and it seems unfeasible to draw the dividing line between one category and another.

A breakthrough in psychology came when Freud emphasized the *developmental* aspects of personality. Man was no longer defined with the notion of "Being" *(Sein)* but with the much more dynamic "Becoming" *(Werden).*[75]

Zurcher's theory[76] of the Self was conceived in the same spirit. He conjectured four main modes or types of the Self. The "A mode" or the "physical Self " is rigid, unsociable, characterised by introspection and reservedness. The "B mode" or "social Self" is stable, relatively static, dependent, concentrates on social questions. The 'C mode" is the "reflexive Self", which is flexible, independent, considers himself as separate from the rest of the society, which he constantly evaluates. And finally the "D mode" or "oceanic or macro-Self" is the extravert, whose main concern is with the universal and transcendental; he appreciates abstract ideas and believes in spiritual-mystical revelations (Kon 147–149). Even though Zurcher's system appears to answer some of our expectations, it would be difficult to try to fit the Zoas into his types. (The physical Self might – warily – be associated with Urizen, while the oceanic Self is a more or less apt summary of the Los of the later Nights.) The main problem with Zurcher's scheme is that he imagines the development of the Self as a progress from "A mode" to "D mode", that is a gradual, chronological improvement. In Blake's poem the heightened awareness of Albion and the Zoas is the result of the interaction of the four characters embellished with the contribution of their Emanations.

Alan Miller's recently elaborated personality typology also differentiates four types (145–218). In his model the four types are defined in terms of analytic-holistic and objective-subjective dimensions, thus he posits the existence of the *objective-analytic* character, whose other denomination is the 'reductionist'; the *objective-holistic* type, who is also called the 'schematist', the *subjective-analytic* or 'gnostic' category, and finally the *subjective-holistic* personality, also denominated as the 'romantic'. (Within each category two subtypes are recognized: the emotionally stable and unstable variants of the main types, thus the essentially fourfold system is extended to an eightfold model.) Mention should be made of a separate type that Miller delineated: the *versatile* type. This comprises individuals who – whenever it is appropriate – are able to adapt both analytic and holistic styles.

---

[74] For a more detailed account of these psychologies see Miller 1–29.

[75] The two principal mechanisms by which development takes place are *identification* and *displacement*. Both notions are beautifully rendered in *The Four Zoas;* the first one in the Orc-cycle, whereby Orc – in the process called "identification with the aggressor" – becomes Urizenic; the second in Los's building of Golgonooza, when he sublimates his frustration and rage at the birth of his son.

[76] For more details see Kon 147–149.

Of Miller's categories[77] two are fairly exact account of Blake's Zoas. The objective-analytic corresponds to (one aspect of) Urizen while the subjective-holistic seems to be applicable to Tharmas.

The objective-analytic type adopts a fairly tough-minded orientation to life ("Listen O Daughters to my voice Listen to the Words of Wisdom / So shall [ye] govern over all let Moral Duty tune your tongue / But be your hearts harder than the nether millstone", Urizen teaches his daughters [VII, 80:110–112]), his central concern is to achieve a control over his environment:

> [Urizen] begun to dig form[ing] of gold silver & iron
> And brass vast instruments to measure out the immense & fix
> The whole into another world better suited to obey
> His will where none should dare to oppose his will himself being King
> Of All & all futurity be bound in his vast chain
> And the Sciences were fixd & the Vortexes began to operate
> On all the sons of men & every human soul terrified
> At the turning wheels of heaven shrunk away inward withring away
> Gaining a New Dominion over all his sons & Daughters
> & over the Sons & daughters of Luvah in the terrible Abyss (VI, 73:229–238)

People in this type want to maintain an emotional detachment because limited emotional involvement eliminates the possibility that one will be influenced by one's own wayward feelings or by the emotional pressure exerted by others. Urizen's chief adversary seems to be Luvah-Orc, who represents passion. They continuously vie with each other until – in Night VII – Urizen seems to be able to subdue him. The emotional detachment that characterizes this type is brilliantly depicted in Urizen's famous sermon:

> Compell the poor to live upon a Crust of bread by soft mild arts
> Smile when they frown frown when they smile & when a man looks pale
> With labour & abstinence say he looks healthy & happy
> And when his children sicken let them die there are enough
> Born even too many & our Earth will be overrun
> Without these arts (80:117–122)

Finally, the objective-analytic type of person typically focuses on the objective world of outward appearances, the external world of physical reality. "As a consequence, a mechanistic world view is developed in which simple cause-effect relationships are sought as a means of understanding and control" (Miller 151). This mechanistic world view is epitomised in Urizen, whose realm is Ulro, which is the world of the "unholy trinity" of Blake: the realm of Newton, Bacon and Locke (with whom Urizen is often associated[78]).

---

[77] For a diagrammatic description of the types see Appendix I.

[78] For Urizen building a Newtonian world see II, 33:271–286. In his famous colour print "Newton", Blake depicts the scientist leaning forward, looking down, his body closely resembling a human brain, domain of Urizen.

The prototypical example of the type is the empirical, impersonal analytical scientist. In Blake's dream this role is cast to Urizen (as one of the interpretations of his name, 'your reason' [Damon, *A Blake* 419], suggests), who created and explored the universe with his "enormous Sciences" (VII, 102:144), and who formed the philosophy of the five senses.

The subjective-holistic type is just the opposite. Its primary concern is with establishing a communion, intimate and nurturing relationships with other people. The members of this category are characterized by a well-developed emotional empathy – concurrently, in *The Four Zoas* Tharmas is the "Parent power" (I, 4:22), and the "Mighty Father" (I, 15:413). When we first meet him at the beginning of the poem he is taking in the Emanations, sheltering them in his bosom because "The Men have recieved their death wounds & their Emanations are fled / To me for refuge & I cannot turn them out for Pitys sake" (4:31–32). In the subjective-holistic type we find a lack of interest in the analysis of personal experience because it is regarded as an alienating experience, another form of separation, which he strives to avoid. This is exactly what Tharmas tells Enion:

> Why wilt thou examine every little fibre of my soul
> Spreading them out before the Sun like Stalks of flax to dry
> The infant joy is beautiful but its anatomy
> Horrible Ghast & Deadly nought shalt thou find in it
> But Death Despair & Everlasting brooding Melancholy
> Thou wilt go mad with horror if thou dost Examine thus
> Every moment of my secret hours (I, 4:48–54)

Because of his basic interest in communion and the aversion to separation, the primary fear of the subjective-holistic people is separation anxiety. We have seen how compulsively Tharmas is seeking his lost Emanation, all his actions in the poem are centered around this search. The defensive reaction to the separation anxiety is the use of unarticulated defences, which in Tharmas's case is to be found in the constant alteration of love and hate he feels towards Enion and his surroundings as well as in his continuous rage, which renders the once "mildest son of heaven" "a terror to all living things" (IV, 49:81–82).

Since – as we have so often emphasized – Blake's Zoas are interconnected, and Miller's model only accounts for two of the four Zoas[79] (Luvah and Los seem to belong to the very broad category of versatile types), for all their similarities, we cannot use Miller's typology to facilitate our understanding of Blake's Zoas.

Blake and Szondi

While the previously studied schemes could only partly correspond to these prerequisites, there seems to be a psychology that shows deep affinities with Blake: Lipót Szondi's depth psychology, designated as the *analysis of vicissitudes* – or simply: fate analysis (commonly known as *Schicksalsanalysis*). Before a detailed comparison of Blake's

---

[79] To be precise, Miller's system describes only one and a half of the Zoas since it does not explain Urizen's double aspect, which we shall discuss later.

and Szondi's notions we shall adumbrate the latter's stance in those four preliminary questions. The most conspicuous similarity between them is that both are based on a primarily fourfold structure, which is extended to an eightfold one. In Szondi's analysis of vicissitudes four basic drives are assumed. These four categories, which he calls "drive-vectors",[80] are the following:

1. *C* vector: contact drive – corresponding to Tharmas
2. *S* vector: sexual drive – corresponding to Luvah
3. *P* vector: paroxysmal (convulsive or startle) drive – corresponding to Urizen
4. *Sch* vector: ego drive – corresponding to Los.

Each of the drives embraces two reaction types, so eight specific drive needs, called "drive factors" can be differentiated (see Appendix II). If our first condition is to be fulfilled then these factors are to be treated as distinct characters. Incidentally, in his foreword to Susan Deri's *Introduction to the Szondi Test,* Szondi appreciatively remarks that the reason the author could understand the eight drive factors so deeply is that "she assimilated the concept, as though the eight factors were in reality eight *living beings* to whom she is eternally bound in friendship" (VII; emphasis added). And indeed Szondi's living beings are very close to Blake's Living Creatures and a closer look at the two formulations will show how the character psychologies of comparable "Quaternals" disclose parallel functions.

Every individual bears inherently all eight basic drive factors, and these factors – it cannot be overemphasized – do not exist *in vacuo.* "They are not static but actively dynamic within a system of dialectic motility" (Szondi–Moser–Webb 18). An individual is qualified by the quantitative variations of these determinants and only their interactions and changes can provide us with valid information on the development of the personality. Since these factors are dependent on the circumstances (both inner and outer) and are constantly modified by their changes (they are *"umwelt-labil"* [Szondi, *Az Én* 194]), any factor in isolation is irrelevant because it can only account for one eighth of the total personality at a given moment. Like the Zoas, the factors are the dramatization of the dynamism of the individuality. (And just like Blake, Szondi is capable of depicting extreme dynamism with the help of his eightfold system, which is further refined: contrast exists not only between the two drive factors within a given drive vector, but each of the factors contains two opposing tendencies, enabling us to follow even very subtle changes in the individual.)

Of the four prerequisites only one remains to be explored: we have to consider whether Szondi's vectors can be regarded as equal or there is a certain hierarchy among them. The ego drive is organically connected to all other drives and has a centralizing function (Szondi, *Az Én* 207), which sets it above the others, but, more importantly, "the ego is the bridge which is capable of spanning all the antithetical poles of the psyche" (Szondi–Moser–Webb 267).

Since the ego drive – as shall be proved later – can be associated with Urthona-Los, its privileged position in the fourfold correlation seems to be in line with Blake criticism.

---

[80] "In mathematics the term 'vector' applies to a complex entity representing directed magnitude. In the same sense, the term 'drive vector' will refer in the experimental diagnostics of drives to a definite drive quantity in a specific drive direction, an entity in which the confluent drive needs and tendencies find expression" (Szondi, *Experimental* 11).

Our contention, however, is that the ego drive (as well as Los) should be regarded as *primus inter pares* which assumption can be substantiated by the fact that the extreme dominance of the *Sch* vector is just as pathological as the extreme prevalence of any other drives. The encroachment of certain tendencies may lead to the disappearance of others and this is the situation Szondi terms "drive peril". In case of drive perils the person is menaced in his unity and defence mechanisms are immediately activated. (Similarly, when Urizen, separated from her Emanation, declares himself God, subdues Orc and seems to gain control over the whole universe by spreading his net of religion, the so-far warring Zoas join forces against him, lest the Eternal Man disintegrate irreversibly.) When it is not counterbalanced by the other three quaternals, the dominance of the ego drive leads to various psychological diseases.

We have seen that a great many of the tenets of Freud and Jung are commonly recognized as capable of offering some creditable interpretations of Blake's poems. Szondi always claimed that his analysis of vicissitudes was the link between these two psychologists; he strove to establish a synthesis between the diverse depth psychological trends by uniting them into an organic whole, in which the personal-traumatic (Freud) and the familial-genetic (Szondi) are merged with the collective-archetypal (Jung).[81] With his intensive research in depth psychology, Szondi intended to place the hitherto occult concept of human destiny upon a medical and psychological basis. For this he elaborated a gene-theory (a synthesis of Freudian psychoanalysis and heredopsychiatry), which has ever since been a subject of debate and has given rise to much controversy. To substantiate this theory he developed his famous test, which became well-known as the "Szondi test"[82]. It revives the age-old theory of physiognomy by assuming that one can determine character by facial appearance. "The entire experimental test is a method for determining relativity in relation to sympathy and antipathy toward the characterologic factors represented by . . . photographs" (Szondi–Moser–Webb 41). Paradoxically, even very recent research in genetics has been unable to prove (or indeed to disprove) the connection between Szondi's test and gene-theory (Bereczkei 152–153; Vargha, *"Újabb adalékok"* 214), upon which Szondi claimed to have based the test. Yet, irrespective of whether or not we accept the medical, theoretical basis of Szondi's postulate, and whether or not we can agree with him in considering his test as being the proper methodology for proving his genetical hypotheses, the Szondi test has stood the test of clinical validity, and has proved itself empirically to be a most useful technique employed worldwide.[83] In our arguments Szondi's theoretical/ genetical hypotheses shall be completely disregarded and it is only the personality typology – the categories and descriptions – of the Szondi test that we shall utilize in our analysis of Blake's figures. It shall be demonstrated that Szondi's drives correspond to the functions personified in the Zoas. Certainly, man cannot be clearly categorized since the categories overlap and change along with the changes in age and development of the individual, but we can always identify the dominance of certain drives, which define the character of the

---

[81] For a comparison of Freudian psychoanalysis and Jungian analytical psychology with Szondi's fate analysis see Szondi, *Módszertan* 299–309. On related matters see also Jamain 181–184.

[82] For the rationale and validitive procedures of the Szondi test see: Deri 6–16; Szondi–Moser–Webb and Lukács, *A Szondi-teszt*.

[83] Today the centre of the Szondian fate analysis is Belgium, where the Szondi test – together with the Rorschach procedure – is effectively used in drawing a mindscape of the personality and with the help of the analysis of vicissitudes psychologists are capable of mapping out the proper treatment of the pathological cases. (This comment is indebted to Dr. Bruno Hilleweare.)

person. As the most remarkable achievement of the test is that it is able to illuminate the basic relationships between the most important tendencies of the human character and is capable of revealing their motion[84] we expect that a collation of Szondi's categories with Blake's Zoas be instrumental in a better understanding of the actions and motivations of the Zoas even when crucial information may be suppressed within the fictional narrative.

Despite the essential similarities between Blake's universe and Szondi's explorations, we certainly cannot claim that there is a one-to-one correspondance. It would be very difficult to prove that the Emanations are always the opposing drive factors; sometimes they mingle, sometimes oppose.

Szondi claimed that in the mentally healthy all the eight drive needs are present in a stable equilibrium. The very same idea is expressed in *The Four Zoas:* each Zoa has his own Emanation or counterpart (they together constitute a drive vector), but once the Emanation is cast out the harmony is broken, the balance is shattered, and Albion gets sick, since what remains of the original unity of the two opposites (or contraries, to use Blake's word) is the Spectre: "The Spectre is in every man insane & most / Deformd Thro the three heavens descending in fury & fire" (I, 5:115-116). It is important to underline that Szondi's drives correspond with the *fallen aspects* of the Zoas – they both describe pathological cases, which in Blake's poem means the allegorical, spiritual sickness of Albion and his indwelling Zoas.

We have found that Blake's mental map is apparently schematized in an analogous if less conscious way than proposed by Szondi. Because Szondi's system was primarily conceived to be of scholarly character and it was composed in the mode of scientific exposition, organised primarily in accordance with scientific principles of structure and discourse – as such it strives to give a detailed analysis of cause-and-effect relation-ships – we expect that it will be a useful tool to complement and illuminate Blake's dream vision.

At this point there might emerge two objections to the collation of Blake's vision and Szondi's ideas. Those who require "influence" as a basis of comparison will find it hard to accept our method. But to quote Martin Bidney's foreword to his outstanding book on Blake and Goethe (between whom – despite the remarkable parallels – no provable influence can be pointed out):

> Those who are interested in deep-rooted affinities between . . . introspective explorers will not be put off. To limit comparative literary study to cause-and-effect relationships is to constrict its scope and impoverish its resources, whereas the challenge of accurately describing spiritual kinships – expressed in similar ideas, myths, and metaphors – offers a stimulus to both the analytic understanding and the synthesizing imagination. (XII)

The other conceivable objection may be based on the fact that in recent years the mathematical and psychometrical analysis of the drive factors of the Szondi test has shown that from a statistical point of view the validity of the respective factors cannot be considered equal; while certain factors are notably consistent (the *h* factor of the sexual drive, for

---

[84] See Vikár 179.

46

example), others are just the opposite (like the *hy* factor of the paroxysmal drive).[85] An introduction of more sophisticated measures and a construction of new personality scales have been suggested to complement the original test.

Just like Freud and Jung, Szondi has been severely criticised and revised in the light of subsequent scientific findings. They all assumed an empirical posture and so subjected themselves to empirical criticism to which they attempted to reply with empirical defenses. Yet, Freud and Jung are not exclusively thought of as natural scientists but also as creators of a new mythology. As Philip Pomper noted, a kind of struggle has been waged over their heritage to determine to which culture they really belong, that of the natural sciences or that of the humanities (21). In Giovanni Papini's mock-interview with Freud, the psychologist "confesses" the following:

> Everybody thinks . . . that I stand by the scientific character of my work and that my principal scope lies in curing mental maladies. This is a terrible error that has prevailed for years and that I have been unable to set right. I am a scientist by necessity, and not by vocation. I am really by nature an artist. . . . And of this there lies an irrefutable proof: which is that in all countries into which psychoanalysis has penetrated it has been better understood and applied by writers and artists than by doctors. My books, in fact, more resemble works of imagination than treatises on pathology. . . . I have been able to win my destiny in an indirect way, and I have attained my dream: to remain a man of letters, though still in appearance a doctor. (Quoted in Hillman 2)

If we considered Szondi, Freud and Jung as scientists only, then their works might indeed call for correction and sophistication. But if we can also see them as works of imagination, as well-developed – unusually logically delineated – mythologies then a much wider scope of possible comparative literary analysis is opened up. This new approach to depth psychology is what James Hillman proposed in 1972:

> I essayed a psychology of soul that is the psychology of the imagination, one which takes its point of departure . . . in processes of imagination. That is a psychology that assumes a poetic basis of mind. Any case history of that mind will have to be an imaginative expression of this poetic basis, an imaginative making, a poetic fiction, disguised . . . in the language of medical science. (4)

It is in this spirit that we shall approach to Szondi's system.

We shall now proceed to examine the characters that inhabit the Albionic – or to use Nelson Hilton's witty coinage: the *All-bionic* (*Some Sexual* 171) – mind. Charu Sheel Singh claimed that a reading of Blake's prophecies makes it clear that his characters are personifications of intellectual qualities. "Their power of appeal does not lie in their resemblance to persons in actual life, but in evoking states of mind with which Blake was actually concerned. They are written not in realistic but in symbolic mode" (137). David Erdman, too, understood Blake's "Visionary Forms Dramatic" as contending perspectives, rather than fully rounded individual characters (quoted in Tannenbaum 48). With the help

---

[85] András Vargha has pursued this question.

of Szondi we shall try to prove that Blake has managed to mingle the realistic and the symbolic and that his characters are life-like individuals – a single character sometimes combining a number of types[86] – even as they are intellectual ideographs.

As has been previously stated, each of the Zoas is assigned a compass point in the Eternal Man's mental map, thus we can establish the following graph:

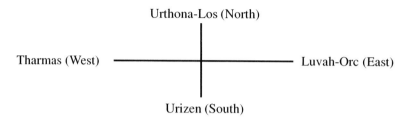

We can see that the result is two axes, the vertical being *Urthona-Urizen*, the horizontal *Tharmas-Luvah;* respectively termed as *Axis of Creativity* and the *Axis of Emotion* (Bidney 111).[87] While primarily Blake's vision was conceived in terms of creative contraries, the basic opposition was between the conceptions epitomized in the figures of Urizen and Luvah-Orc (he is called Fuzon in *The Book of Ahania*), with Los depicted as a complementary character to Urizen, when the essentially bipolar myth was extended into a quadripolar one, the reason-passion dichotomy was counterbalanced. As Martin Bidney asserts, with Tharmas and Urthona the poet introduced models of self-transcendence; the fourfold vision was designed, "from the allegorical perspective, to counter each of the champion self-affirmers, the Passionate Striver Luvah . . . and the Intellectual Urizen . . . with a contrary force capable of exemplary self-transcendence, namely Compassion or Intuition (Tharmas) and Transcendent Imagination or Loving Creativity (Urthona)". With the new mapping proposal the two self-affirmers were no longer to be constantly opposing each other, since both acquired a "morally contrasting contrary" (Bidney 108, 110), that is a self-transcending contrary. (Strangely enough, even though Urizen and Luvah are certainly contrasting in their temperament, their self-affirmations show a lot in common.)

Martin Bidney's Axis of Emotion and Axis of Creativity seem to correspond perfectly with Szondi's differentiation between the *border* (comprising the contactual and sexual) and the *middle* (containing the paroxysmal and ego) drives. The method of the border and the middle was developed to analyse the dialectic movement between the border drives and the drives of the middle. Szondi has designated the middle as the censorial system;

---

[86] Blake's use of typology as intellectual shorthand has already been referred to. Even as he uses paradigmatic events from the Bible he employs character typology. "Los in *The Book of Urizen* represents Jehovah, Adam, Abraham, Apollo, Hephaestus, Jeremiah, Laius and Jupiter. . . . Also, like biblical figures, Blake's characters are often corporate personalities, representing both individuals and classes of individuals, much as someone like Esau or Edom is both a person and a nation" (Tannenbaum 118).

[87] Hume, on the other hand – following Jung – suggests that the most basic oppositions are between imagination versus sensation (Los vs. Tharmas) and reason versus passion (Urizen vs. Luvah) [250]). Wilkie and Johnson put forth yet another proposal. They claim that the Zoas function as two pairs: a primary system of antagonistic opposers (Urizen and Luvah-Orc) and a secondary or responsive system of compatible potential allies – Tharmas and Los, responding independently to the chaos brought forth by he other pair. The latter two are sometimes capable of coordination and cooperation (115).

that part of the personality which is concerned with the individual's system of values, his attitudes and his orientation toward life (Szondi–Moser–Webb 12; Lukács, *Szondi* 73). Since – as has already been adumbrated and shall be proved shortly – the contactual drive is analogous with Tharmas, the sexual with Luvah, the paroxysmal with Urizen and the ego drive with Urthona-Los, the Axis of Emotion can also be called "the border", while the Axis of Creativity "the middle." The reason why we shall prefer the terms used by Szondi is that they more aptly express the relative importance of Urizen and Urthona-Los in the regeneration of Man.

Jacques Schotte, the most influential Szondi disciple of the day, has based his Theory of Circuits *(Théorie des Circuits)* on Szondi's differentiation of the border and the middle, and has proposed that in the drive scheme a certain order may be postulated. The order of the drives, *from the simplest to the most complex* is as follows: Contact-Sexual-Paroxysmal-Ego drives.[88] As it has been found that the Zoas of Blake's myth "adhere to" Schotte's Theory of Circuits the discussion of the characters shall follow this proposed order, with the only exception that – for practical purposes – Urizen/paroxysmal drive shall be examined last. Since it is in the understanding of Urizen's character that we dissent most from Blake scholarship, he shall be considered finally, in the light of his three fellow Zoas.

Before the analysis of the role of the respective Zoas in *The Four Zoas,* we shall try to undecipher the names of the Living Creatures which will be followed by a brief summary of their previous occurrance in Blake's poetry. (The term 'Zoa' is used here to express the unity of male and female components, so under each Zoa his Emanation will also be discussed.) The reason we examine the etymology of the names of the Zoas is that the strange nomenclature seems to carry essential information on their bearers.[89] According to Daniel Stempel, Blake's naming – unlike that of Adam's – is *re*naming.

> It is not the creation of *lingua adamica* in a brave new world but the retrieval of a lost language, a *lingua aeterna* in a fallen world. His names are pieced together from the ruins of the languages of Babel, fragments scattered over the earth by the wanderings of people and the fall of empires in postdiluvian history. What appears to be arbitrary combinations of letters and syllables are Blake's reconstruction of a lost original, reaching back beyond the history of linguistic change to that language of Eternity in which word and thing are identical, "visionary forms dramatic". (95–96)

Stempel claims that the names of the Zoas themselves reflect the breakup of the *lingua aeterna,* since 'Tharmas' seems to be derived from the Anglo-Saxon *thearmas,* 'bowels'; "Luvah" from the Hebrew root for the heart or passions: *lv* or *lvh;* Urizen from the Greek *ourizein,* 'to limit'; and finally "Urthona" from *urdd,* the Welsh word for 'honour'. While Stempel's argument is indeed appealing, it cannot be substantiated with irrefutable textual evidence therefore his speculations shall be complemented with other conceivable explanations in the case of the respective Zoas.

Our first subject of analysis is the drives of the border, Tharmas and Luvah.

---

[88] Lecture delivered by J. Schotte at the Centenary Szondi Conference, 14 April 1993, and Van Meerbek 185.

It is important to emphasize that the order he has proposed does not imply value judgement, it simply refers to the complexity of the individual drives.

[89] For related matters see: Fogel; Hilton, *Literal*; Spector. Fogel considers Blake's names as pictures-in letters, Spector examines their Hebraic origin and background, while Hilton studies their linguistic features.

CHAPTER II

THARMAS AND ENION

> *So long as we were mere children of nature, we were*
> *both happy and perfect; we have become free, and*
> *have lost both. . . . Strive for unity, but seek it not in*
> *uniformity; strive for repose, but by means of*
> *equilibrium and not of the cessation of your activity.*
> *That nature which you envy in the non-rational is*
> *unworthy of your respect or longing. It lies behind*
> *you, it must ever lie behind you.*
>
> *Schiller*

The names Tharmas and Enion may be derived from Thaumas and Eione (Frye, *Fearful* 284), who are Hesiod's sea god and shore goddess in the *Theogony*. This seems all the more possible as fallen Tharmas sinks into the Sea of time and space and is associated with water all through the poem: "the World of Tharmas, where in ceaseless torrents / His billows roll where monsters wander in the foamy paths" (II, 33:256–257). Furthermore, Thaumas is the father of Iris, the rainbow, which signals the end of the flood; similarly Tharmas's daughter, Enitharmon, is the main agent of the Apocalypse and regeneration.[90]

As David Erdman pointed out, the names 'Tharmas' and 'Enion' appear to be the back formations from the name of their daughter: Eni-Tharmon (*Prophet* 275). Although we cannot substantiate our hypothesis with a reference from the texture of the poem, it does not seem impossible to conjecture another etymology for Enion's name. Just like the name 'Enitharmon' suggests her filial relationship to Enion and Tharmas (this suggestion is confirmed several times in the poem, as the conception and birth of Enitharmon is repeatedly described[91]), similarly, we could confer that the name 'Enion' implies that she is a daughter of Eno and Albion. Since Eno (possibly an anagram of *eon*) is the "aged Mother" (*BoL* plate 3), the mother of all poetry (*FZ* I, 3:6) and Albion is the Universal Man, it is quite likely that the Emanation of "Parent power" Tharmas is their offspring.

Neither Tharmas nor Enion appear in Blake's poetry before *The Four Zoas*. We first meet them in the midst of a marital quarrel, which starts the poem. Enion is jealous of Jerusalem – Albion's Emanation and the bride of Jesus who comprises within herself all the Emanations, just like Albion is the composite form of all humanity – and of the Emanations whom Tharmas has sheltered in his bosom out of compassion. In the ensuing conflict they sunder, and as the primeval connection between them disintegrates, they are both doomed to fall. No longer the bucolic characters "of the sort that the wheels of history run over: good but not too bright, easily confused" (Ostriker 159), their relationship perverts into a sado-masochistic one, and Enion weaves the Circle of Destiny out of Tharmas's fibres:

> [Tharmas] sunk down into the sea a pale white corse
> In torment he sunk down & flowd among her filmy Woof
> His Spectre issuing from his feet in flames of fire

---

[90] In Night II, Enitharmon is likened to a "bright rainbow weeping & smiling & fading" (34:382).
[91] I, 7–8:185–192; IV, 50:84–106; VII, 84:277–295.

In gnawing pain drawn out by her lovd fingers every nerve
She counted. every vein & lacteal threading them among
Her woof of terror. Terrified & drinking tears of woe
Shuddring she wove – nine days & nights Sleepless her food was tears
Wondering she saw her woof begin to animate. & not
As Garments woven subservient to her hands but having a will
Of its own perverse & wayward Enion lovd & wept
Nine days she labourd at her work. & nine dark sleepless nights
But on the tenth trembling morn the Circle of Destiny Complete
Round rolld the Sea (I, 5:77–89)

Confronted with the Circle of Destiny, the Daughters of Beulah close the Gate of the Tongue, which provides an entrance from Ulro to Beulah. The allegorical meaning of the tongue (sense of Tharmas) was illuminated by Northrop Frye, who pointed out that eating the body and drinking the blood of Jesus is a profound image of the final apocalypse, so taste (tongue) implies our imaginative control of this world. "Just as sight is the mind looking through and not with the eye, so taste is the mind transforming food, and thus 'taste' in the intellectual sense is the mental digestion of the material world. Tharmas, then, is the tongue of unfallen man, his power to absorb the nonhuman" (Frye, *Fearful* 281). When the Gate of Tongue is closed, Tharmas sinks into the chaos of Ulro. In the primordial unity of Eternity Tharmas was "darkning in the West" (I, 4:22), which – from *Tiriel* on – has been the realm of the body. Since the instinctual unity of the body (depicted in the figure of Tharmas), which once comprehended and held together all the other faculties, has fallen into chaos, the disintegration of these faculties is also inevitable.

Almost completely simultaneously with Blake, young Schelling, in his insightful essay *On the Origin of Human Evils in the Most Ancient Philosophy of Genesis, Chapter III* (1792), formulated contentions strikingly similar to the ones delineated in *The Four Zoas*. Drawing heavily on Lessing, Herder and Kant, Schelling asserted that in Eden – just like in the golden age of myths – man was under the dominion of his senses, instincts and the rule of necessity; even as the primordial unity of the Zoas was presided over by Tharmas. From this state of innocent ignorance, Schelling argues, man was driven by the urgency of reason, so *homo sensibilis* was confronted by *homo intelligibilis* and instead of happy obedience man was reduced to the misery of knowledge, which in the end – albeit through perilous paths – will necessarily lead to man's maturity.[92]

Concurrently, the central trope of *The Four Zoas* is life as a circuitous pilgrimage from the realm of Tharmas to the reign of real Humanity.

In the vision of the fall the poem dissents considerably from the notions of *The Book of Urizen*. While in *The Book of Urizen* the cause of the fall was Urizen's self-assertion and the fall of the rational faculty/Urizen inevitably brought about the fall of the poetic imagination/Los, in *The Four Zoas* the Fall is depicted from several points of view, and we are left in doubt as to whether it was Urizen or another Zoa who has brought about the disintegration of Albion into bellicose members. What is certain is that the disruption of the original unity first effects Tharmas, who is the first one to fall. The fall of the senses

---

[92] For a more detailed discussion of the topic see Abrams 218–219.

and of the instinctual unity of the body then brings about the fall of the other Zoas which points to the heightened significance of the Parent Power as well as to the crucial role of the – so far rejected – senses as inevitable to sound mental functioning.[93]

Fallen Tharmas begets time and space (Los and Enitharmon) on Enion, who is soon deserted by the children. She starts out to find them, "In weeping blindness stumbling she followd them oer rocks & mountains" (I, 9:215) all in vain, just like she is sought after by Tharmas all through the nine nights to reunite with him only in the apocalypse. The wanderings of Enion and Tharmas coincide with Man's fall from Innocence, his tribulations of going through Experience. Indeed, Tharmas's and Enion's bewildered panic to find out what has happened to them goes hand in hand with the reader's disintegration and panic (due to the complete abandonment of sequential narrative, whose calming effect is widely recognized) to locate himself in the strange world of the poem.

Although in the major part of the poem we face the *fallen* Tharmas, emblematic of the horrors of sundered existence, from the regularly recurring nostalgic accounts of Eternity we learn that he once presided over Beulah ("in those blessed fields / Where memory wishes to repose among the flocks of Tharmas" [II, 34:326–327]), which is the idyllic (or quasi-idyllic) world of pastoral harmony, presented in the *Songs of Innocence:*

> Art thou O ruin the once glorious heaven are these thy rocks
> Where joy sang in the trees & pleasure sported on the rivers
> And laughter sat beneath the Oaks & innocence sported round
> Upon the green plains & sweet friendship met in palaces
> And books & instruments of song & pictures of delight (VI, 72–73:212–216)

While in his unfallen form Tharmas is the Good Shepherd, the disintegrated Zoa (also called the Spectre of Tharmas) seems to be the precise negation of his previous self. After his fall is completed in Night I, Tharmas's actions are conditioned by his futile yearning after Enion. His sado-masochistic repulsion of his consort in Night III, his bidding Los to rebuild the universe (so that he can destroy it), his separation (which he immediately regrets) and subsequent unification of Los and Enitharmon in Night IV, his suicidal "pact" with Urizen to end his torments in Night VI, his punishment of his enemies, an ambiguous deed of revenge (which paradoxically signals the nearing apocalypse) in Night VII, his relegating his power to Los in Night VIII, and his rebirth as a child in the pastoral interlude of the last night as well as his final reunion with Enion followed by his active participation in the apocalypse are all but complementary to, and conditional upon his main activity: his search for his lost ideal, Enion– which is indeed a search for his lost self.

Since – as we have noted – Szondi's categories and descriptions have many affinities with the fallen aspects of Blake's Living Creatures, we shall proceed to examine the separated Tharmas and Enion with an eye on Szondi's system. While in his eternal form Tharmas is Compassion now he has become its opposite: wrath and violence. The reason for this change is the frustrated search after Enion, which renders him a good example of Szondi's *Category of Everlasting Loneliness and of Hypomania* of the contact drive. In

---

[93] The fact that Tharmas is the most susceptible to changes may imply that something has been preserved of the former contention about the frailty of senses.

members of this category, Szondi notes, the separation of the person from his love object "makes for a distractable, unstable, restless disposition" (*Experimental* 192) – as it is manifested in many cases (especially in Night IV) by Tharmas's inability to hold on to his ideas, decisions: "he reard his waves above the head of Los / In wrath. but pitying back withdrew with many a sigh / Now he resolvd to destroy Los & now his tears flowd down" (48:45–47). Just like in Szondi's category people feel a compelling need to search for the lost ideal and "the hopelessness and disappointments of this activity . . . generate self-hatred, self-torture and depression" (*Experimental* 193), Tharmas is a pathetic figure, constantly brooding over his sundered counterpart in self-abasement[94]:

> Fury in my limbs. destruction in my bones & marrow
> My skull riven into filaments. my eyes into sea jellies
> Floating upon the tide wander bubbling & bubbling
> Uttering my lamentations & begetting little monsters
> Who sit mocking upon the little pebbles of the tide
> In all my rivers & on dried shells that the fish
> Have quite forsaken. O fool fool to lose my sweetest bliss
> Where art thou Enion ah too near to cunning too far off
> And yet too near (III, 44-45:162–170)

But the masochism of Tharmas soon turns into sadism,[95] both against Enion, whom he cruelly repels: "I send thee into distant darkness / Far as my strength can hurl thee wander there & laugh & play / Among the frozen arrows they will tear thy tender flesh" (III, 45:170–172) – just to regret it and fall into an even deeper despondency – and against his environment, as it is clearly indicated by the fact that while in Eternity he was the unifying power, in Night IV he tears Los and Enitharmon apart, inflicting grinding pain on them. Ironically, he immediately repents of his cruel deed and commands the separated Spectre to reunite them, threatening him with rending him asunder in bloody tortures ("thy limbs shall separate in stench & rotting & thou / Become a prey to all my demons of despair & hope" [IV, 49:74–75]) if he should not obey his will. The sadism of these people, Szondi claims, is an expression of the person's desperate hatred, rage and vindictiveness against the world from which – in the absence of the beloved one – he feels separated forever (*Experimental* 192–193).

---

[94] Enion experiences the same feelings; she blames herself for her jealousy and accuses herself of being the prime agent of their separation ("do thou [Tharmas] / Thy righteous doom upon me", "Tho I have sinned. tho I have rebelld / Make me not like the things forgotten as they had not been"; [III, 45:186–187, 191–192]), and sinks into deep dejection projecting a very debased image of herself:

> I am made to sow a thistle for wheat; the nettle for a nourishing dainty
> I have planted a false oath in the earth, it has brought forth a poison tree
> I have chosen the serpent for a councellor & the dog
> For a schoolmaster to my children
> . . . .
> My heavens are brass my earth is iron my moon a clod of clay
> My sun a pestilence burning at noon & a vapour of death in night (III, 35:387–396)

[95] The drive for clinging [Tharmas], Szondi notes, seems to be organically connected to sadism and a thirst for power. The need for separation and search [Enion] is just the opposite; there is in these people a tendency to self-denial and masochism (*Módszertan* 284).

(Tharmas's vindication of the role of God shall be referred to later).

Tharmas laughd furious among the Banners clothd in blood
Crying As I will I rend the Nations all asunder rending
The People, vain their combinations I will scatter them
. . . .
In war shalt thou bear rule in blood shalt thou triumph for me
Because in times of Everlasting I was rent in sunder
And what I loved best was divided among my Enemies
. . . .
Therefore I will reward them as they have rewarded me
I will divide them in my anger & thou O my King
Shalt gather them from out their graves & put thy fetter on them
And bind them to thee that my crystal form [Enion] may come to me
(VII, 96:49–51; 97:59–60, 69–72)

But for all his hostile attitude towards his environment, Tharmas does not transfer his murderous impulses into action and discharges his accumulated rage in furious speeches and threats. The reason seems to be the same as in the case of most people in this category: they "have become too restless and distracted to concentrate their hatred upon one object sufficiently to be ready to kill him" (Szondi, *Experimental* 193). When Tharmas encounters Urizen in Night VI, he offers him a suicide pact: "Withhold thy light from me for ever & I will withhold / From thee thy food so shall we cease to be" (69:64–65), but Urizen does not even bother to reply to him. Outraged Tharmas threatens to kill him, but paradoxically what he menaces to do is exactly the same as what he offers in the pact: he will deprive Urizen of food and indulge in the horrible consequences: "Thou shalt pursue me but in vain till starvd upon the void / Thou hangst a dried skin shrunk up weak wailing in the wind" (69:70–71).

It is crucial to recognize here, that however chaotic and distraught Tharmas may be in his fallen form, he has – as the pact proves – unconsciously retained the intuition of the essential interconnectedness and unity of the Zoas, and is dimly aware that intellect has to feed upon instincts, just as without the light of intellect the senses were unable to function properly.

But more importantly, this suicide pact signals a landmark in Blake's visionary universe. The possible allience and thus dropping out of reason and senses is refused here, indicating that these two functions – praised so highly by the Enlightenment – gained firm footing in Blake's system of values as indispensable to Man's regeneration. At this point the poem seems to share Bacon's concern who in the *Great Instauration* set out to investigate "whether that commerce between the mind of man and the nature of things . . . might by any means be restored to its perfect and original condition," through establishing "forever a true and lawful marriage between the empirical and rational faculty, the unkind and ill-starred divorce and separation of which has thrown into confusion all the affairs of the human family"(quoted in Abrams 60). The passage of the suicide pact eloquently disproves George Saintsbury's assertion that "in no contemporary – not in Coleridge himself – is the counter-creed to that of the Neo-classics formulated with a sharper precision, and withal a greater width of inclusion and sweep"(3: 269).

We have seen that Tharmas's conflict with Urizen came from the latter's refusal of a mutual suicide. Paradoxically, immortal Tharmas desires the death of his undestructable body.[96] His powerful death instinct, which we encountered as early as the beginning of Night IV, is the result of his antithetical feeling of hope and despair. "The realization that the truly desired object may not be found leaves the individual with an utter indifference. He evaluates available value objects with the standards of one who is prepared to die" (Szondi, *Experimental* 193).

> Ah Enion Ah Enion Ah lovely lovely Enion
> How is this All my hope is gone forever fled
> ....
> Deathless for ever now I wander seeking oblivion
> In torrents of despair in vain.
> ....
>   When dark despair comes over [me] can I not
> Flow down into the sea & slumber in oblivion. Ah Enion (IV, 47:8–23)

But the death impulses are just one way of coping with the absence of Enion. Sometimes it seems that Tharmas abandons the search for his consort and instead of the adherence to his unobtainable ideal he indulges in completely different activities – which as a rule finally turn out to be vaguely, sometimes almost inexplicably, connected to his search – like the commissioning of Los to rebuild the universe in Night IV, immediately after he uttered his desire to be dead. Tharmas wants a world to rule over, a realm that he can destroy ("renew thou I will destroy / Perhaps Enion may resume some little semblance / To ease my pangs of heart & to restore some peace to Tharmas" [48:55–57]). This coincides with what Szondi calls megalomaniac phase, an exaggerated feeling of power during which the search is replaced by hasty casting about without goal or focus; a passing phase because of the instability of acquisitive impulses (*Experimental* 192–193). Whatever is attained is soon cast aside as without worth. Similarly, Tharmas declares himself God, but immediately (fifteen lines later!) relinquishes his claim: "Is this to be A God far rather would I be a Man" (51:146) to repeatedly call himself God ten lines later.[97]

To sum up fallen Tharmas's characteristics we can conclude that he is a raging, sado-masochistic figure, incoherent, inchoate, and chaotic, a ghost of that human integral that he was in his eternal existence. At this point it would be all too easy to dismiss him as a pathetically dependent, inconsistent, irresolute creature (his element is water, which is rather difficult to visualize, liquid and not solid, lacking the bounding outlines, whose importance in painting is forever stressed by Blake[98]), weak and frail, in whom the ever-recurring depression hinders all actions, a late-comer in Blake's poetry who apparently was only conceived to complete the fourfold scheme and to accentuate the striking

---

[96] "For death to me is better far than life. death my desire / That I in vain in various paths have sought but still I live" (VI, 69:58–59).

[97] To this aspect of Tharmas, Robert Jay Lifton's description of the schizophrenic is especially apt: "The schizophrenic experiences a pathetic illusion of omnipotence, a despairing mask of pseudo-immortality because he is blocked in the most fundamental way from authentic connection or continuity – from what I have been calling a sense of symbolic immortality. He therefore fantasizes omnipotence & pseudo-immortality. But the productions of the schizophrenic are infused with death: . . . he sees himself as dead, other people around him as dead, the world as dead" (286).

[98] *A Descriptive Catalogue of Pictures* and *Annotations to the Works of Sir Joshua Reynolds*.

difference between him and Los, the Eternal Prophet, to whom – somewhat unaccountably – he finally delegates his power in Night VIII. But we should be wary of drawing such a one-sided conclusion. A closer look at Szondi's description of Tharmas's category which has so far seemed to be consistent even in the subtlest details – we learn from Szondi that the most important socially positive occupation that the members of the category tend to choose is painting (*Módszertan* 65), just like Tharmas's art is painting in the fourfold correlations – warns us that the contact drive and its categories may carry much more significance than it appears at first sight. Szondi points out that the contact drive (consisting of factors *d* and *m*) has a central role in the individual in that certain drive factors (the *h* and *s* of the sexual drive – Luvah; and the *e* and *hy* of the paroxysmal drive – Urizen) can only function when connected to the contact drive (*Módszertan* 278–279).

We shall examine whether the correspondences between Szondi and Blake hold true in this point; whether Tharmas's central role can be substantiated from the texture of *The Four Zoas*. There are two explanations that offer themselves.

1. We have seen that the basic conflict between Tharmas and Enion was the result of Tharmas's hiding the fleeing Emanations in his bosom. Since the Emanations represent the creative power of humanity that is preserved during the fall, Tharmas, who is the repository of this crucially important power, assumes a special significance. This notion is in accord with the idea, which became a commonplace by the Renaissance and which Milton put forth in *Of Education,* that after the Fall divine truths could be communicated to man through the senses. So also, in biblical prophecy, which was a major source of inspiration to Blake's vision, the Holy Ghost, like Tharmas, is acting as a painter (Tannenbaum 58), a motif probably not accidental in the poem.

Paradoxically, as Tharmas laments in Night VII, his sheltering the Emanations led to the separation from his own Emanation, Enion, and resulted their fall:

> My little daughters were made captives & I saw them beaten
> With whips along the sultry sands. I heard those whom I lovd
> Crying in secret tents at night & in the morn compelld
> To labour & behold my heart sunk down beneath
> In sighs & sobbings all dividing till I was divided
> In twain & lo my Crystal form that lived in my bosom
> Followd her daughters to the fields of blood they left me naked (VII, 97:60–66)

2. The other important instance is the fact that the Circle of Destiny is drawn from his fibres[99] which would suggest a negative role of Tharmas, as the turning of the Circle implies an even deeper entanglement in the material world, but it shall be pointed out later that the immersion in the totality of experience is a prerequisite to the regeneration of the Universal Man, a prevailing idea that lay in the public domain of Western culture at Blake's time.

John B. Pierce attributes a most significant role to Tharmas. According to him Tharmas is not only instrumental in bringing about and carrying out the redemption of Albion, but he is Albion himself:

---

[99] As Nelson Hilton so convincingly proves in his remarkable article "Some Sexual Connotations", the fibre refers to the semen, as it is appropriate in the case of Tharmas, Parent power.

The weaving imagery . . . suggests Tharmas's incarnation into the limitations of the physical body, while the notion that he holds the emanation Jerusalem within suggests the potential for redemption of the body when it contains the city of God. These associations suggest that Tharmas is analogous to the universal human form of the One Man, Jesus Christ. Such associations give Tharmas a symbolic equivalence with Albion. (100)[100]

While Pierce's arguments in connection with the role of Tharmas in *Jerusalem* seem well-grounded, the identification of Tharmas and Albion in *The Four Zoas* appear to be a conclusion he drew in the knowledge of the later epic, and not so much from the text of the poem in discussion. We would rather urge another interpretation that assigns Tharmas a similarly important role.

In Night IV Los triumphantly declares that even though his God is Urizen (traditionally identified with the God of the Old Testament), he is fallen into the deep "And Los remains God over all" (48:41). Knowing that Los is Imagination, that is Jesus Christ, we can take his words as the indication of the coming of the rule of Jesus. This assumption is supported by Tharmas's response: "Doubting stood Tharmas in the solemn darkness" (48:44), where the doubting Tharmas may be taken as an ingenious pun subtly referring to the doubting Thomas of the Bible, who needed tangible proof of the resurrection of Christ. Once the biblical connotation has been established in the doubting Thomas-Tharmas intimation, the substructure of the poem calls for further associations. Suffering from the fierce pangs of the ambiguous feelings of love and rage, Tharmas denies Los three times, (IV, 49:53–55; 51:131–132; 52:156), just like Peter denied Jesus[101]. The Tharmas-Peter parallel is strenghtened by the fact that while Peter had to confess his love to Jesus three times consecutively (John 21:15–17), similarly, Tharmas relegates his power to Los thrice in three consecutive nights (VII, VIII and IX). We learn from the Bible that Peter is the rock upon whom Jesus's church is built, against which the gates of hell cannot not prevail, and Peter is given the keys of the gate to the kingdom of heaven (Matthew 16:18–19). In *The Four Zoas* Los builds Golgonooza (City of Art, the New Jerusalem in Blake's poetry in which the "Divine Countenance shone" [VIII, 100:40]):

> For now he feard Eternal Death & uttermost Extinctiom
> He builded Golgonooza on the Lake of Udan Adan
> Upon the Limit of Translucence then he builded Luban
> Tharmas laid the Foundations & Los finishd it in howling woe (V, 60:75–78)

The parallel is striking: just like Jesus's kingdom is built to overcome eternal death, Golgonooza is erected to serve the same purpose. While the first is raised over the rock – Peter, the second is founded by Tharmas. (Similarly, in the last night Los fights his battle leaning over Tharmas, just like resurrection in Jesus is made possible for us with the help

---

[100] He goes on to argue that the suggestion that Tharmas became a model for Albion can be an explanation for the Zoa's relative absence from *Jerusalem.* To prove this assumption he brings four examples: 1. On Plate 25 of *Jerusalem* Albion's fibres, like Tharmas's, are drawn out by a female figure to create the vegetated world. 2. Albion's Spectre moves to the west, which is Tharmas's realm. 3. While in *The Four Zoas* Tharmas hides Jerusalem, in *Jerusalem* this is done by Albion. 4. Certain lines that are addressed by Enion to Tharmas (*FZ* I, 4:33–36) are given over to Vala to direct to Albion (*J* Plate 22:1, 10–12).

[101] Urthona-Los's words to Tharmas could have been addressed by Jesus to Peter: "wherefore shouldst thou rage / Against me who thee guarded in the night of death from harm" (*FZ* IV, 50:109–110).

of his earthly governor, Peter.) Peter has the keys to heaven, Tharmas is the keeper of Luban, the Gate of Golgonooza, the gate of salvation which opens into our world.

When Peter remedies his denial of Jesus by three times confessing love, he is commanded to feed Jesus's lambs and sheep,[102] and thus from the fisherman he becomes the shepherd that tends Christ's flock. Tharmas, once a water god, whose body surged forth in fish (VI, 69:61), is regenerated at the end of the Apocalypse as a shepherd: "Tharmas brought his flocks upon the hills & in the Vales / Around the Eternal Mans bright tent the little Children play / Among the wooly flocks" (IX, 138:838–840).

Szondi's assumption that the contact drive/Tharmas is vital to the proper functioning of the sexual/Luvah and paroxysmal/Urizen drives substantiates the Peter-Tharmas hypothesis, as the latter two are closely connected to, and may be interpreted as, (one aspect of) Jesus and (the Old Testament) God.

For a Peter-Tharmas association to be plausible one would expect Tharmas to have an underlying innocence in his nature. The fact that he is the only Blakean Quaternal never to be associated with Satan, a very complex state of error, death, war and selfishness, seems to answer this expectation. As Wilkie and Johnson put it: "it corroborates our impression that although human instinct can become chaotic, weak, and misdirected, it is incapable of the absolute error to which more complex faculties are susceptible" (181–182).[103] It is also important to note that he is the only one of the four Zoas who is reborn as a child before the resurrection.

But this child is no longer the child of "The Little Boy Lost" and "The Little Boy Found" of the *Songs of Innocence,* the dependent infant, who is desperately lost without his parent, whom any darkness can vapourize leaving the child helpless again,[104] but much rather the child of "The Land of Dreams" of the Pickering Manuscript:

> Awake awake my little Boy
> Thou wast thy Mothers only joy
> Why dost thou weep in thy gentle sleep
> Awake thy Father does thee keep
> O what Land is the Land of Dreams
> What are its Mountains & what are its Streams
> O Father I saw my Mother there
> Among the Lillies by waters fair
> Among the Lambs clothed in white
> She walkd with her Thomas in sweet delight
> I wept for joy like a dove I mourn
> O when shall I again return
> Dear Child I also by pleasant Streams
> Have wanderd all Night in the Land of Dreams
> But tho calm & warm the waters wide

---

[102] John 21:15–17 ("So when they had dined, Jesus saith to Simon Peter, Simon, *son* of Jonas, loveth thou me more than these? He saith unto him, Yea, Lord; thou knowest that I love thee. He saith unto him, Feed my lambs.")

[103] The only thing we cannot accept from this observation is that Tharmas is regarded as an essentially simple character. What we are trying to prove is even the opposite: the intricacy of his personality.

[104] I am following Harold Bloom's interpretation of the two poems (*Blake's* 47).

I could not get to the other side
Father O Father what do we here
In this Land of unbelief & fear
The Land of Dreams is better far
Above the light of the Morning Star

Although the imagery, the mood and the obvious biblical allusion to the ideal Beulah world of the twenty-third Psalm would render the poem to belong to the pastoral lyrics of the *Songs of Innocence,* there seems to be a crucial difference between them. Little Thomas (Tharmas), who now lives in the land of unbelief and fear, is pining for the Land of Dreams, but what sets this land apart from the land of innocence is formulated in the last line: it is "Above the light of the Morning Star". As is well-known, the Morning Star, Lucifer, is associated with Urizen (as the first is "the light-bearer", the second is the "Prince of Light")[105] the light is the light of his intellect. The fact that the child aspires after an idyllic land, but one which is intricately connected to the realm of Urizen, suggests that little Thomas is the rejuvenated Tharmas of Night IX, who has gone through the horrors of disintegrated existence, and even though he has retained his innocence, he is now conscious of the importance of suffering and experiences in order that a higher ontological state, a more aware consciousness, an organized innocence may be achieved by the Eternal Man.[106]

As has been pointed out, our contention is that Tharmas is much more complex a figure than he may seem at first sight. Of all the Zoas he seems the least likely to share any characteristics with Urizen, and yet there are sophisicated hints of their similarities. (It is important to emphasize that their similarities pertain to their fallen form.) The inconstancy and capriciousness of Tharmas – his raging outbursts, which are always followed by his regret and atonement – is strikingly similar to the two alternating aspects of Urizen which in Szondi's terminology are called the Cain and the Abel phases. An evidence of the analogy between the two Zoas is to be found in the fact that it is Urizen that Tharmas offers a suicide pact; he intimates their intricate resemblance and suspects that Urizen's death is essentially his as well. More straightforward than this is the association of Tharmas with doubt while elsewhere we are directly advised that "Urizen who was Faith & Certainty is changd to Doubt" (II, 27:105). The last night of *The Four Zoas* brings about a significant transformation in all the Quaternals but it is only Urizen and Tharmas who are rejuvenated: the hoary Urizen as a radiant Apollo, Tharmas as an innocent child. Finally, the strong link between the two Zoas is evidenced by the essential interconnectedness of their

---

[105] Two more evidences for the Morning Star-Urizen association may be cited: 1. Lucifer is the first of the seven Eyes of God, the first step in the fall from the original unity, on the path of Experience. The disintegration of the Zoas is blamed on Urizen, who initiated the fall by attempting to usurp Urthona's place thus causing a war. 2. Urizen's lament at having failed to obey the divine word which led to his fall from Eternity clearly echoes the casting out of Satan in *Paradise Lost*:

I went not forth. I hid myself in black clouds of my wrath
I calld the stars around my feet in the night of councils dark
The stars threw down their spears & fled naked away
We fell. (*FZ* V, 64:222–225)

[106] Jung traces the same idea in the Bible in Jesus's words: "Except ye be converted, and become as little children, ye shall not enter into the kingdom of heaven" (Matthew 18:3). These children, Jung explains, are born from the experiences of maturity; and are aware of the necessity of the opposites within (*Válasz* 115).

Emanations. They both are relatively insignificant as far as the frequency of their presence in the poem is concerned. But as a rule, when they appear, the emergence and actions of one effects the future of the other. Enion's lament in Night II, her powerful death instinct irresistably pulls down Ahania, who sinks into a deadly sleep and disappears from the scene until the eighth night, when she bewails the state of the disintegrated Man. Her lament is answered by the now hopeful Enion, who consoles Ahania by prophecying the coming of the Saviour. The faith of Enion prepares the way for the reunion of Ahania with Urizen, which in turn, leads to the long-sought resurrection of Tharmas and Enion.

The determinig part of Urizen in the regeneration shall be analysed in a later chapter, but we can already conclude that Tharmas's association with him, together with the Parent power's other aspects delineated above, point to Tharmas's potential importance as a kind of encompassing power, essential to the substucture of the poem.

CHAPTER III

LUVAH AND VALA

The death of one god is the death of all.
Wallace Stevens

The name 'Luvah' is most often regarded as a derivation from "love" or "lover", as befits the Zoa of Passion. Martin Bidney suggests that the name may also imply "lava" (106) probably referring to the heat and bursting energy of emotions. Luvah's counterpart is Vala, who was originally to be the main character of the poem as the first title suggests. There have been several attempts at deciphering her name, the most common of which seems to be the notion that it can be traced back to "veil", an implication of her elusiveness (e.g., Damon, *A Blake* 432). (In *Jerusalem* she is often referred to as a veiled beauty: "Vala replied weeping & trembling, hiding in her veil" [20:11].) Alicia Ostriker suggests further associations; she conjectures that the word "veil" as the source of Vala's name is a reference to the membranous "veil" which preserves virginity as well as to the "veil" covering the tabernacle of the Old Testament, as she "stands at the intersection between corrupt sexuality and institutional religion"; she is Fortuna, Babylon, the Great Whore, the chaste mistress and femme fatale, the like of whom is mainly to be found in French literature (in Gautier and Baudelaire) and in the figures of Swinburne and Shakespeare (160). The problem with these interpretations (together with the other prevailing explication of the etymology as Vala = vale, the valley of shadow and death) is that they concentrate exclusively on the *fallen aspect* of the Emanation, while in her fallen form, Vala is very often distinguished as "the Shadowy Female" or "Rahab" or "Mystery" (VII, 93:224; VIII, 106:329–330). Much more sophisticated is Northrop Frye's suggestion – which accounts for both the fallen and unfallen perspectives of Vala – according to which her name is that of the Scandinavian prophetess and guardian spirit of the earth in the *Völuspa* in the Elder Edda (*Fearful* 270).

Luvah is mentioned first in *The Book of Thel*[107] ("O virgin know'st thou not. our steeds drink of the golden springs / Where Luvah doth renew his horses") where he represents innocent sexuality, and does not return until *The Four Zoas,* in which we first meet his Emanation, Vala. Under different names, however, they are both known from the earlier poems; Luvah as Orc while Vala as the Shadowy Female.

Orc is the fallen aspect of Luvah. His story is fully depicted in *The Four Zoas* but a great part of it is adumbrated in *The Marriage of Heaven and Hell, America, Europe* and *The Book of Urizen*. He is "Blasphemous Demon, Antichrist, hater of Dignities; / Lover of wild rebellion, and transgresser of Gods Law" (*America* Plate 7), which makes him a chief antagonist of Urizen. All these characteristics explain his name, which is probably derived from 'orcus', as his prime identity, his abundant energy, is often assigned to the

---

[107] He might also be associated with "the prince of love" of "How sweet I roam'd from field to field" of the *Poetical Sketches*.

realm of hell. The name is also an anagram for 'cor', heart, which refers to his connection to Luvah.

The Shadowy Female is the fallen form of Vala and her story, too, is sketched in the earlier poems of *America* and *Europe,* but her character is hardly as elaborated as Orc's, her consort's. We know that she is Enitharmon's daughter, sister and lover to Orc, principle of fertility; an ambiguous woman, in whose figure the nascent concept of the Female Will is foreshadowed, but who is also a redemptive force in that she can foresee the apocatastasis. (This double nature of the female, as destroyer and preserver, will be typical of all the Emanations.) Just like Orc's, her story, too, is expanded in *The Four Zoas.*

Of all Blake's Zoas (and indeed of all the figures in Blake's mythology) Luvah has created the greatest controversy and confusion as he is the "figure through whom Blake primarily expressed his own imaginative breakthroughs, and he embodies all the ambivalence of an initial stroke of vision" (Altizer, *History* 78). The complexity of this most elusive character is manifested in the fact that he is depicted as three different figures, who are yet one and are simultaneously present in the poem. The unfallen aspect of Luvah seems to be almost completely absorbed by Jesus, the fallen one by Orc, while the Zoa under the name of Luvah may stand for both these aspects. According to Wilkie and Johnson two conceivable explanations for Luvah's lack of definition as a character suggest themselves.

> One is the obvious artistic problem of representing love in a way that will appear neither to aethereally sacred nor too earthily profane to a fallen audience. . . . The second explanation has to do with the relation between energy [Orc] and love [Luvah] in Blake's evolving mythology. . . . Whether Blake intended all along to identify Luvah with Orc or whether in reconsidering his own view of Christianity he came to see hatred and lust as perverted forms of love, Blake makes Orc a vivid personage but keeps Luvah's character shadowy, implying that there is something inexplicable about the redemptive action of love. (44)

In the following chapter we shall examine the actions of Luvah-Orc-Jesus with the intention of trying to find an answer to the apparent vagueness of the character. The entanglement of the narrative shall necessitate a somewhat more detailed description of their story.

We first encounter Luvah and Vala in Enitharmon's account of the fall in Night I: "Luvah and Vala woke & flew up from the Human Heart / Into the Brain; from thence upon the pillow Vala slumber'd. / And Luvah siez'd the Horses of Light, & rose into the Chariot of Day" (I, 10:262–264).[108] As we learn later, Luvah's usurpation of Urizen's place (man's emotional life against his intellect) was one of the prime reasons for the sickness of Albion, as the ensuing warfare led to the fall of the Zoas. In this account Blake yet again dissents from *The Book of Urizen* inasmuch as Urizen, who was there the main culprit is now depicted as a victim of aggression.

The messengers of Beulah relate the story from a somewhat different perspective: Urizen wants to conspire with Luvah to gain dominion over Man, offering Luvah his own realm, himself trying to occupy Urthona's domain:

---

[108] Luvah's seizure of the Sun, a version of the Phaetan myth, was already adumbrated thirty years before in "How sweet I roam'd from field to field" of the *Poetical Sketches.*

do thou alone depart
Into thy wished Kingdom where in Majesty & Power
We may erect a throne. deep in the North I place my lot
Thou in the South listen attentive. In silent of this night
I will infold the Eternal tent in clouds opake while thou
Siezing the chariots of the morning. (I, 21:489–494)

Although Luvah refuses the pact, he seizes Urizen's chariot, and as a consequence there starts a bloody war in which the Emanations flee to Tharmas and – as has been described in the previous chapter – disintegration begins. Luvah and Vala feel triumphant, unaware that the fall of Tharmas will inevitably bring about their fall as well. For a while it seems that Luvah has managed to gain dominion over Albion, who – mistaking him with Urizen – worships him as God (III, 40:48–66). But as Albion realizes his mistake, he indignantly puts forth Luvah from his presence and casts both Luvah and Vala out: "And as they went in folding fires & thunders of the deep / Vala shrunk in like the dark sea that leaves its slimy banks / And from her bosom Luvah fell" (III, 42:102–104). Their separation is precipitated by the fact that the dying Albion resigns his rule to Urizen ("Take thou possession! take this Scepter! go forth in my might / For I am weary, & must sleep in the dark sleep of Death / Thy brother Luvah hath smitten me but pity thou his youth" [II, 23:5–7]), who casts Luvah into his furnaces of affliction and completely melts him (an indication of the repression of emotions by reason) to build the Mundane Shell upon the ashes (of passion). To further complicate the story of the fall of Luvah and Vala, it turns out in Night VII (a typical prequel) that Vala seduced Albion and became pregnant with Urizen:

Vala was pregnant & brought forth Urizen Prince of Light
First born of Generation. Then behold a wonder to the Eyes
Of the now fallen Man a double form of Vala appeard. A Male
And a female shuddring pale the Fallen Man recoild
From the Enormity & calld them Luvah and Vala. (83:244–248)

The birth of Urizen, then, seems immediately to bring about the separation of Luvah and Vala, while earlier we were told that Urizen's (thwarted) conspiracy with the then-unfallen Luvah led to the latter's disintegration. This seems to suggest that Urizen's birth is coincidal with his existence.

With the division (fall) of Luvah and Vala now consummated, there is a significant change in their character. Once lover and beloved, the Eros and Psyche in Man, now they have turned into their opposite: "I was love but hatred awakes in me" (II, 27:104). Simultaneously with the transformation of the Prince of Love, however, Jesus puts on Luvah's robes of blood, "[l]est the state calld Luvah should cease" (II, 33:264), a motive, whose significance is underlined by the fact that it is repeated several times in the poem like a textual refrain. When in the furnaces of affliction Luvah is melted (and Vala's fire with which she feeds the furnaces die out), the reader would expect that he disappears from the scene. This expectation seems to be supported by the fact that "the Eastern vacuity the empty world of Luvah" (VI, 71:156) is now a horrid bottomless void. Yet, conversely, not only is Luvah's role taken on by Jesus, but – with a Blakean twist in the narrative – he is also reborn as Orc from the heart of Enitharmon (another possible source for the name as the anagram of 'cor'). As his conception – he is begotten immediately after the fall of his parents – so is his birth: "The groans of Enitharmon shake the skies the labring Earth / Till from her heart rending his way a terrible Child sprang forth / In thunder smoke & sullen flames & howlings & fury & blood" (V, 58:36–38). The birth of Orc plants jealousy into his father's heart and as the child grows up, Los can no longer curb his jealousy, which he so far has tried to sublimate by building Golgonooza. What follows is the most beautiful rendering of the phenomenon, which Freud came to call "the Oedipal conflict", in poetic terms. (It is important to note here that while for Freud the Oedipal conflict is primarily a crisis for the child, Blake adheres to the original myth, in which aggression starts with the parent's fear of his offspring. In both of Blake's minor prophecies, *The Book of Urizen* and *The Book of Ahania,* where he develops this theme, he is true to the myth.)

> But when fourteen summers & winters had revolved over
> Their solemn habitation Los beheld the ruddy boy
> Embracing his bright mother & beheld malignant fires
> In his young eyes discerning plain that Orc plotted his death
> Grief rose upon his ruddy brows. a tightening girdle grew
> Around his bosom like a bloody cord. in secret sobs
> He burst it, but next morn another girdle succeeds
> Around his bosom. Every day he viewd the fiery youth
> With silent fear & his immortal cheeks grew deadly pale
> Till many a morn & many a night passd over in dire woe
> Forming a girdle in the day & bursting it at night
> The girdle was formd by day by night was burst in twain
> Falling down on the rock an iron chain link by link lockd
> . . . .
> Calld it the chain of Jealousy. (V, 60:79–95)[109]

With the chain of Jealousy Orc is nailed to the rock, an interesting motive simultaneously referring to the myth of Prometheus and foreshadowing the death of Jesus in Luvah's robes of blood. Even though Los repents his horrible deed, he cannot free his son as the chain has strucken root into the rock and become one with Orc, a living chain sustained by his life. Just like Luvah before, Orc has been repressed, and thwarted energy rages now in vain in front of his arch-enemy: reason. For Urizen descended into the caves of Orc out of pity with the intention of teaching him his wisdom.[110] Orc passionately rejects him, and in his answer to Urizen he dramatically establishes himself as completely opposite to the

---

[109] Based on this conflict, Aaron Fogel put forth yet another possible reading of the name "Orc': Orc's chains . . . are pictured in the *Zoas* as having been created out of Los's sobbing: each sob is described as a *cord* around Los's chest that bursts, each burst band becoming one of the links in Orc's youthful bondage. . . . The name 'Orc' itself, looked at as a kind of picture-in-letters, could be drawn as a complete circle followed by two broken or semi-circles: a small chain. . . . Orc's name both as sound and as picture-in-letters evokes the abrupt, the truncated, the broken-off. In the story of the chains and their origin, Blake implies that the word 'cord' recoiled to form the name 'Orc' itself, so that 'Orc' contains, represses, in its abruptness, a kind of involuted or twisted grief. Revolutionary anger is described as solidified mourning" (223).

[110] Abrahams identifies Urizen's motives as fear because, as he says, "the state of Orc exists always where art or freedom is suppressed and is thus a constant source of fear to tyrants" (51).

Prince of Light (VII, 78–79:28–89). He is enchained, burning with fierce energy, flaming in fury, young and restless, while Urizen is free yet sitting still, obdurate, aged, hoary and as cold as hail. Orc's defying Urizen is so intense that one is reminded of the notion of "conflictual undifferentiation" formulated by René Girard (in connection with Shakespeare): "The more our characters tend to see one another in terms of black and white, the more alike they really *make* one another. . . . The more these characters deny the reciprocity among them, the more they bring it about, each denial being immediately reciprocated" (quoted in Bidney 129–130).

A cogent testimony for Orc's mistake in regarding himself as completely different from Urizen is revealed by Orc himself: "I well remember how I stole thy light & it became fire / Consuming. Thou Knowst me now O Urizen Prince of Light" (VII, 80:147–148). This speech of self-revelation establishes Orc as reborn Luvah; the Promethean youth is identical with the Prince of Love. The light that becomes fire consuming may be seen as a reference to the myth of Prometheus as well as an ingenious reminder of Luvah's seizure of Urizen's horses of light which led to his consummation in the fires of the furnaces of affliction. What happens here is strikingly similar to what Gaston Bachelard termed as the *Promethean complex*. He pointed out that the *Promethean complex* is a tendency to know as much as – or more than – our fathers, to apprehend as much as – or more than – our masters, in other words, the *Promethean complex* is the Oedipal complex on the intellectual plane (26–27). Luvah's intention to usurp Urizen's domain expresses his desire to know as much as him, to become intellect, an eloquent proof that not only does he not consider themselves incongruous, he even wants to become identical with his quasi-opposite. A similar tendency is discernible in the case of Orc facing Urizen in Night VII; Orc is unable to resist Urizen's wisdom: "thou beginnest to weaken / My divided Spirit Like a worm I rise in peace unbound / From wrath Now When I rage my fetters bind me more" (80:135–138), and (in the process that in psychoanalytical terminology is called "the identification with the aggressor") Orc becomes entirely Urizenic, "turning affection into fury & thought into abstraction" (80:155) to finally put on a Serpent body and be crucified on the Tree of Mystery.

Different as his arguments may be, Martin Bidney comes to a similar conclusion:

> As he eats the bread of affliction, Orc's serpent-body breaks out in a rash of gems, symbolic of his solidifying ideas and lordly ambitions: "the pestilential food in gems & gold / Exuded round his awful limbs" . . . . This is Blake's striking allusion to God's denunciation of the King of Tyre in Ezekiel: "every precious stone was thy covering . . . they have filled the midst of thee with violence, and thou hast sinned . . . and I will destry thee, O covering cherub, from the midst of the stones of fire" (Ezekiel 28:13, 16). By presenting snaky Orc as "covering cherub" like the Tyrian monarch, Blake is suggesting that Orc, too, would gladly found a Urizenic empire if he had the chance. Orc begins to look like a mirror image of his detested rival, Urizen. (130–131)[111]

The birth of Orc goes hand in hand with the appearance of Vala as the shadowy female, who cumulatively represents the single vision of Ulro and the double vision of Generation (Verma 201). The changes that have taken place in their characters (compared to their

---

[111] In similar vein Frye, *Fearful* 210 and Hilton, *Blake* 86–87.

role in the earlier myths) are significant. We have seen how Orc gradually becomes a complementary figure to Urizen; a similar process is discernible in case of her consort: "Earlier the Vala-figure was the gaoler's daughter of folk-tale and myth, an Ariadne who helps the liberating hero and, becoming his lover, is liberated by him" (Fuller 135). In *The Four Zoas* the 'nameless shadowy Vortex' is the main instrument of Orc's repression. Her motives are clearly stated: "With sighs & howling & deep sobs that [Orc] might lose his rage / And with it lose himself in meekness she embracd his fire" (VII, 90:127–128).[112] Of the passionate lover she becomes a tyrant, and "the constant mixture of military and sexual violence in the poetry surrounding her and her pleasure in violence of which she is the source also associate her with Urizen" (Fuller 135).

We have seen that Luvah has so far been destroyed twice and so by the eighth night, with the crucifixion of Orc – or in other words: his assimilation into Urizen at the end of a process that Frye termed the Orc-cycle – all that Luvah once stood for appear to have been eliminated. Yet, providentially one aspect of his remains: that which was taken on by Jesus.

> When Urizen saw the Lamb of God clothed in Luvahs robes
> Perplexd & terrifid he Stood tho well he knew that Orc
> Was Luvah But now he beheld a new Luvah. Or One
> Who assumd Luvahs form & stood before him opposite (101:61–64)

Just like in the previous nights, there is a confrontation between Luvah and Urizen and Urizen yet again manages to win: in the antepenultimate night Christ incarnated in Luvah is crucified. Simultaneously with the incarnation of Jesus we face the transformation of Vala into Rahab, a member in the Synagogue of Satan.

It would appear that with this third aspect of Luvah eradicated (together with the complete deterioration of his Emanation) we witness the ultimate victory of Reason over Passion, but the poem is more complex than that. Luvah's total extinction is prevented – thus his reappearance in Night IX is made possible – by two circumstances. 1. As the climax of the Orc-cycle in Night VII, Orc organized a Serpent body. The fact that this ultimate state of Orc is depicted as a serpent subtly implies that this state is to be preserved from complete disappearance, since the serpent – a most complex symbol – does not only stand for its most immediate connotation as 'evil' or 'tempter', but is also emblematic of immortality, as it can slough its skin and so perpetually regain its youth.[113] 2. Luvah's rendering as the incarnation of Christ is also suggestive of transcendence as the crucifixion of Jesus symbolizes the death of his *physical* aspect only, and not the extinction of the totality it represents. The motives of Orc's turning into a serpent and Luvah's crucifixion as Jesus, then, explain what otherwise would seem inexplicable: how it is possible for Luvah – after the destruction of all three of his forms – to reappear in Night IX.

In the apocalypse we see all the three aspects of the Zoa of Passion mingled together. Orc now burns in raving fire, but as his rage is no longer curbed by Urizen, who is ordered by the recuperating Albion to "Let Luvah rage in the dark deep even to Consummation / For if thou feedest not his rage it will subside in peace" (120:142–143), he soon burns

---

[112] For a detailed discussion of this transformation see Hagstrum.
[113] For the positive aspect of the serpent see Raine, *Blake* 1: 236–240 and Santarcangeli 225–227.

himself out. As the consummation of Orc is complete, Luvah and Vala take over the place of Orc and Rahab, who no longer appear in the poem (thus the triple aspect of Luvah is reduced to a twofold one, containing only Jesus as an extra layer over the original Zoa). Albion gives Luvah and Vala into the hands of Urizen, who assigns them a new place: "return O Love in peace / Into your place the place of seed not in the brain or heart" (126:364–365). With the Zoa of Passion in the loins, the brain is re-established as Urizen's domain, while the heart is now ready for the reception of resurrected Tharmas. As the human integral is now almost resumed, Luvah and Vala reassume their eternal form as lover and beloved and in a pastoral interlude they are born into Beulah, Vala's Garden of innocence.

> Invisible Luvah in bright clouds hoverd over Valas head
> And thus their ancient golden age renewd for Luvah spoke
> With voice mild from his golden Cloud upon the breath of morning
> Come forth O Vala from the grass & from the silent Dew
> Rise from the dews of death for the Eternal Man is Risen
> She rises among flowers & looks toward the Eastern clearness
> She walks yea runs her feet are wingd on the tops of the bending grass
> Her garments rejoice in the vocal wind & her hair glistens with dew (126:385–392)

The bucolic setting and Vala's answer are reminiscent of *The Book of Thel,* but while Thel failed to enter the world of experience, regenerate Vala is more like Oothoon, Thel's redeeming contrary, in that she consciously descends into the valley and plucks its flowers and fruits, symbolic references to resurrected sexuality.[114]

It is customary to consider this interlude as a moment of unclouded happiness.[115] Yet, beautiful and reassuring this scene may seem among the tumult of the final night, a closer reading of the text reveals that this is not yet the final, ideal state for Luvah and Vala. Vala's Garden is

> The land of doubts & shadows sweet delusions unformd hopes
> They saw no more the terrible confusion of the wracking universe
> They heard not saw not felt not all the terrible confusion
> For in their orbed senses within closd up they wandered at will (126:379–382)

Their unawareness of the pain of the apocalypse that surrounds them and the closed senses strongly suggest a state similar to prenatal existence, a reading in which Vala's

---

[114] Our understanding of Oothoon's sexuality is in line with the most representative trend in the interpretation of *Visions of the Daughters of Albion,* put forth by Erdman, Bloom and Ostriker. Laura Haigwood in her thought-provoking essay, "Blake's *Visions of the Daughters of Albion*: Revising an Interpretive Tradition" challenges this interpretation of Oothoon's sexuality and sees it as much more sinister and ambiguous than critics claim it to be.

[115] This pastoral idyll in the midst of the upheaval of the Apocalypse may recall Schiller's idea of the path to a higher innocence, formulated in *On Naive and Sentimental Poetry.* In this immensely influential essay Schiller exhorts the poet "not to lead us back to our childhood" but to "lead us onward to our coming of age, in order to allow us to feel the higher harmony which rewards the fighter and blesses the conqueror. Let him set himself the task of an idyll . . . which will lead mankind, for whom the way back to Arcadia is closed forever, onward toward Elysium" (quoted in Abrams 215).

Garden may stand for *hortus conclusus*, "closed garden", in medieval works symbolic of the Virgin Mary's womb. "Even when his language recalls pastoral and hymn, even as he soothes us . . . Blake lulls us into a false sense of security. . . . Perhaps in *The Four Zoas*, Vala's Garden, veiled in darkness belongs more to the shadowy dead than the living lovers. Elysian Fields are beautiful, but for all that in Hades" (Haigney 117).

Still, the reunion of Luvah and Vala has a redeeming effect, Urizen "Cried Times are Ended he Exulted he arose in joy he exulted / He pourd his light & all his Sons & daughters pourd their light / To exhale the spirits of Luvah & Vala thro the atmosphere" (131:568–570). The reconciliation of reason and passion finally takes place. "Luvah's liberation is precisely what is accomplished in Night IX of *The Four Zoas*. As he drinks the 'wine of ages' and sings a new song, '[h]is crown of thorns fell from his head' Luvah has ceased to define himself in opposition to Urizen; he has realized that Urizen is a 'Man' and not a 'God'" (Rosso 186). The falling off of the crown of thorns is also symbolical of the termination of the double aspect of Luvah; he is no longer to be associated with Jesus but has regained his original, undivided essence as one of the Quaternals. The reconciliation of Luvah and Urizen is mutual: Urizen, who has so far treated Luvah as his principal victim, no longer strives to subdue him and has learned to accept his fellow Zoa as an indispensable agent of the apocalypse. Luvah's task is to gather the vintage. With an interesting shift in tone the pastoral world of Luvah and Vala now turns into a wild orgy of exuberant joy ("How red the Sons & Daughters of Luvah how they tread the Grapes / Laughing & shouting drunk with the odors many fall oerwearied / Drownd in the wine is many a youth & maiden") and pain ("But in the Wine Presses the Human Grapes Sing not nor dance / They howl & writhe in shoals of torment in fierce flames consuming" [136:743–745; 748–749][116]). The previous aspects of Luvah as a god dying for mankind (Jesus), and demigod suffering for humanity (Prometheus-Orc) are now transformed into a completely different one: Luvah has become a Dionysian wine-god. It seems that instead of atoning for the world, Luvah and his rule now inflict pain on their victims:

> They Dance around the Dying & they Drink the howl & groan
> They catch the Shrieks in cups of gold they hand them to one another
> These are the sports of love & these the sweet delights of amorous play
> Tears of the grapes the death sweat of the Cluster the last sigh
> Of the mild youth who listens to the luring songs of Luvah (136–137:767–771)

What we witness here is the result of the repression of emotions in the previous nights. Just like the energy of Orc before, by the end of the apocalypse the passions of Luvah and Vala are consumed in the bacchanalic intoxication, frenzy and violence, and the Zoa, who at first may have seemed the most likely to produce the Messiah, has become "dung on the ground" (137:791)[117] to fertilize the ground before Urthona-Los.

---

[116] For those who see the pastoral interlude as an ideal – final – state for Luvah and Vala this shift in tone may seem unaccountable but once we accept it as a step in the culmination of error it is intelligible.

[117] The death of the corporeal, physical aspect of Luvah must be annihilated before Albion may assume his truly Human form, as "hell is the being shut up in the possession of corporeal desires which shortly weary the man for *all life is holy*" (*Annotations to Lavater's 'Aphorisms on Man'*).

The portrayal of Luvah in *The Four Zoas* is almost like a palinode of formerly cherished 'Romantic' ideas about the supremacy of passions. In the poem – simultaneously with the inclusion of the senses into the pantheon and the changed appreciation of the role reason – Luvah/passion is assigned a far less leading position.

> Considered ideally, these two – the Zoa of love and his consort – possess attractiveness and grace. But there is a clear indication that their position is not the highest, the myth placing them more often than not in positions of service. All this, of course, befits a faculty or an appetite that is a part not the whole, that is powerful but not supreme, and that is gracious only when it is subordinate. Luvah and Vala in great eternity are not mighty monarchs but gentle angels ranged in order serviceable. It is important to stress the qualities of gentle subservience ministering to harmony and proportion in the ideal state, because in the fallen state these beings assume the opposite characteristics. They become raging tyrants – burning, destroying, dominating. (Hagstrum 38)

After summarizing the main actions of Luvah and Vala in the poem, we shall now examine how their characters correspond to Szondi's descriptions. The category that they seem to be most apt examples of is the *Category of Dual Unionism* – or in other words: the category of the unsatisfied sadistic impulses (Noszlopi 99) – of the sexual drive. This assumption seems to be substantiated by the Luvah-lava [l ∧v∧] reading of the Zoa's name as it is then the mirror image of Vala.

Just like the members of this category cannot function without their partner, needing his/her continued presence, Luvah and Vala also seem to be inextricably bound to each other:

> But Luvah & Vala standing in the bloody sky
> On high remaind alone forsaken in fierce jealousy
> They stood above the heavens forsaken desolate suspended in blood
> Descend they could not. nor from Each other avert their eyes (I, 13:359–362)

But they are doomed to separation, and as we have seen, their sundering brings about a complete transformation of their characters. Szondi's investigations have shown that "if the dual union is disrupted, repressed aggressions may be aroused and the person may become vengeful" (*Experimental* 183). This is exactly what happens to Vala after she is rent from Luvah; when his separated consort is cast into Urizen's furnaces of affliction, she willingly assists Urizen and feeds "in cruel delight, the furnaces with fire" and "[i]n joy she heard his howlings" (II, 25:73; 26:78). She retains this cruelty all through the poem and exhibits violence and malevolance towards all three aspects of Luvah. Luvah himself cannot escape the effects of the breaking up of the original integrity, from love he now turns to hate and in a beautiful lament he relates the birth and death of their dual union:

> in times of Everlasting
> When I calld forth the Earth-worm from the cold & dark obscure
> I nurturd her I fed her with my rains & dews, she grew
> A scaled Serpent, yet I fed her tho' she hated me
> Day after day she fed upon the mountains in Luvahs sight
> I brought her thro' the Wilderness, a dry & thirsty land

And I commanded springs to rise for her in the black desert
Till she became a Dragon winged bright & poisonous
I opend all the floodgates of the heavens to quench her thirst
And I commanded the Great deep to hide her in his hand
Till she became a little weeping Infant a span long
I carried her in my bosom as a man carries a lamb
I loved her I gave her all my soul & my delight
. . . .
And they have taken her away & hid her from my sight (II, 26–27:82–98)[118]

Luvah's song and his brooding over the loss of Vala is very similar to what we have seen in the case of Tharmas. According to the findings of the Szondi test the categories of Tharmas ("everlasting search") and Luvah ("dual unionism") are psychologically closely related. (Szondi, *Experimental* 183). In the subsequent nights not much is revealed about Luvah's attitude to Vala because it is his dying-god aspect that is emphasized. More is disclosed about Vala; she does not give herself up to depression but – as typically done by people in this category – apparently takes revenge by seeking new partners and establishing promiscuous relationships (Szondi, *Az ember meghatározása* 73) – or at least this is what Orc is led to believe: Orc was "Silent as despairing love & strong as Jealousy / Jealous that she was Vala now become Urizen's harlot / And the Harlot of Los & the deluded harlot of the Kings of Earth" (VII, 91:136–138).

Picture 3 The Whore of Babylon (watercolour, 1809)

---

[118] Blake provides a striking illustration of the transformation of Vala. "Vala as dragon and as harpy-vulture-mermaid with emphatically drawn genitals depicts the corruption of sexual life into something cruel, brutal, devouring. The partially erased marginal drawings, a woman hugging a bat-winged phallus and a moth-winged woman with abnormally large breasts, make a similar point: the corruption of Luvah signifies the birth of pornography" (Fuller 103–104).

This degenerated, sadomasochistic relationship that resulted from the separation of Luvah and Vala cannot be ameliorated until their reunion, which takes place in the pastoral interlude of the last night (in which Blake gives a detailed description of their now-idyllic relationship).[119]

We may wonder why the fallen Luvah and Vala are depicted as characters that are bound together in a dual union. Our contention is that the inextricable relationship of Luvah and Vala is subtly ironical, as it shall be proved that Luvah is the historical (physical) aspect of Jesus, while Vala stands for the Church, which – to Blake's abhorrance – came to worship the past and particular body of Christ, and became bound to the mere remembrance of the dead body of Jesus, believing that the literal body that perished on the cross and the sepulcher is the foundation of Christianity[120] thus turning the Christianity of the soul into the Churchianity of outward religion and ignoring the spiritual aspect of the descent of the Messiah, which is the only valid interpretation of his incarnation. The first part of our hypothesis is substantiated by the fact that Jesus's descent and/or suffering and crucifixion in Luvah's robes of blood is unmistakably emphatic in the poem: "Eternity appeard above them as One Man infolded / In Luvah[s] *robes of blood & bearing all his afflictions*" (I, 13:363–364); "And the Divine Vision appeard in Luvahs *robes of blood*" (II, 32:247 – repeated twice in the next few lines); "Saviour (...) / Appearest clothd in Luvahs *garments*" (IV, 56:254–258 – already stated nine lines earlier); "They vote the *death* of Luvah & they *naild him to the tree* / They *pierced him with a spear & laid him in a sepulcher*" (VIIb, 92:166-167); the motif of Jesus assuming a dark Satanic body and putting it off on the cross is reiterated all through Night VIII (nine times):

> The Lamb of God descended thro the twelve portions of Luvah
> Bearing his sorrows & rec[iev]ing all his cruel wounds
> Thus was the *Lamb* of God condemnd to *Death*
> They *naild him upon the tree of Mystery* weeping over him
> And then *mocking* & then worshipping calling him Lord & King   (105–106:323–327)

until finally in Night IX "His *crown of thorns* fell from his head" (135:711; all emphases are added). The metaphor of Jesus descending in Luvah's robes of blood all too clearly refers to the incarnation as Christ's putting on a vegetated body; so also the emphasis on the crucifixion and the cross signify the *mortal* death of Jesus.[121] Another proof for the

---

[119] Their relationship is idyllic (as they are reunited), just the circumstances will have to be changed.

It would be tempting to add one more point of analogy to our comparison, as the assertion that "the loss of the partner" in subjects of this category "may be reacted to by excessive drinking" could well correspond to the orgy of the last night, but by the time of the bacchanal Luvah and Vala are already reunited. Another enticing point of comparison presents itself in Szondi's observation that after the disruption of the dual union, members of the category may attempt to comfort themselves by striving for purity and atonement. Purity and atonement, of course, would seem to perfectly fit in with Luvah's Promethean-, and Jesus-aspects but we must remember that Luvah was forced to undergo the afflictions, and his sufferings (which are usually associated with the atonement) were not his conscious choice.

However, to mention a valid parallel as well, we would like to draw the attention to the fact that according to Szondi one of the most frequent pursuits in the category is to be a musician which is in harmony with Blake's association of Luvah with music (Szondi, *Experimental* 183–184).

[120] For a discussion of related matters see Altizer, *The New Apocalypse*.

[121] In the 1809 illustration of *The Last Judgement* (Rosenwald Collection) Blake no longer depicts the cross as exulted into Heaven; it is falling headlong – with the serpent wound about – into the abyss.

claim that in Luvah we are presented the physical body of Christ can be found in the fact that the Zoa corresponding to him in Ezekiel is the ox or bull (we have allusions to the "bulls of Luvah" in Nights II, V, VII and IX). In the Luvah-bull association not so much to the strength of passions is implied (as for this implication the other Zoa-animal, the lion, would be much more appropriate, being not only mighty but also untamed), but much rather the notion of Luvah as a sacrificial victim.

Nancy M. Ide's computer analysis of *The Four Zoas* also supports our argument. She claims that

> the overall pattern of alternation between areas of high and low image density, affects the reader's perception of the poem. . . . A reduction in imagistic connotations places more emphasis on narrative meaning. . . . The text segments characterized by low image density are, for the most part, more plot oriented than the sections of the poem containing the densest concentrations of imagery. (*Image* 128–129)

As we can see in her graph (Appendix III), the image levels reach their lowest point in the middle of Night VIII; here the imagery becomes so sparse that – because of the almost total lack of imagistic meaning – our attention is exclusively drawn to the act itself, obviously yielding it a heightened significance. What happens, then, in the climactic passages of the eighth night. The middle sections of the night are devoted to the description of the crucifixion of Jesus, but even more crucial than that (as Christ's death on the cross was already related in the previous night so this in itself would not account for the increased importance of the passage) is that we learn at this point what happens *after* the crucifixion: Jesus's dead body is taken off of the cross to signal the beginning of a mistaken worship of his physical aspect:

> Jerusalem saw the Body dead upon the Cross She fled away
> Saying Is this Eternal Death Where shall I hide from Death
> Pity me Los pity me Urizen & let us build
> A Sepulcher & worship Death in fear while yet we live
> Death! God of All from whom we rise to whom we all return
> And Let all Nations of the Earth worship at the Sepulcher
> With Gifts & Spices with lamps rich embossd jewels & gold (106:331–337)

As the poems prove, Blake did not deny the significance of the crucifixion, but his idea of it was completely different from that of the Church, whose "cruciolatry" (Damon, *A Blake* 84), worship of death and materialism he could not accept. The crucifixion is regarded as an *internal* event, taking place in every man when he casts out his Selfhood (this is what *The Everlasting Gospel* of 1818 is about) and assumes his true spiritual body. *The Four Zoas* testifies that the Lamb of God descended "To put off Mystery *time after time* & as a Man / Is born on Earth so was he born of Fair Jerusalem / In mysterys woven mantle" (VIII, 104:263–265 – emphasis added). The significance of the crucifixion is precisely in the fact that Jesus had "first to Give his vegetated body / To be cut off & separated that the Spiritual body may be Reveald" (VIII, 104:266–267). This is certainly not a once-for-all event so the Church's confinement to the mere remembrance to the past and particular body of Christ is a destructive error, for when the death of Jesus is known only as an event of the past, it cannot be repeated as an eternal and universal occurrence.

The fact that the death of Luvah (whose identity with Jesus is so painstakingly emphasized all through the nine nights) is related several times in the poem may be seen as Blake's ingenious way of expressing his rejection to accept Christ's death as an event that took place once, at one particular time in history.

Of the many subtle hints scattered in the poem which suggest that Luvah is the historical aspect of Christ, one shall be explored that is connected to Luvah-Orc. In Night VII we learn from Vala that Orc (who hides Luvah) "torments me for Sin / For all my Secret faults which he brings forth upon the light / Of day" (94:249–251). This avenger is certainly not Blake's real Jesus, whose religion is the Forgiveness of Sin, but much rather the Son of God, who came to promulgate the Decalogue. In Blake's oeuvre, however, the Ten Commandments were abhorred abstract rules that "no flesh nor spirit could keep" (*BU* 23:25), as they imposed general regulations on the particular individuals, and he saw in them the culmination of materialism:

> Thus the terrible race of Los & Enitharmon gave
> Laws & Religions to the sons of Har binding them more
> And more to Earth: closing and restraining:
> Till a Philosophy of Five Senses was complete (*SoL* 5:13–16)

The only ethics Blake could accept was embodied in the Everlasting Gospel, and the only Jesus that he recognized as the true Messiah was the Antinomian Christ of this gospel. The idea of the Everlasting Gospel, which lies at the centre of Blake's thought, goes back to the 12th century Italian mystic, Joachim of Flora. He taught that history fell into three great periods: 1. ordo conjugatorum (the Age of the Father, Old Testament) 2. ordo clericorum (the Age of the Son, New Testament) 3. ordo monachorum (the Age of the Holy Spirit). The first period was characterized by fear and servile obedience, the second by faith and filial obedience, while the last, Joachim believed, would be the age of love and spiritual liberty ("Joachim of Flora"; Reeves passim). The visible Church of the second age was to be absorbed by the spiritual Church of the third, and the historical Jesus (remembered by Christendom) – the cultic Christ of *The Four Zoas* – was to give way to the epiphany of the universal Divine Humanity.

> In the coming age of the Spirit the full truth of the Everlasting Gospel will be revealed, not in a new sacred book but in a new revelation of the spiritual sense of the Bible with which God will illuminate the hearts of men. In this age God will be within man and therefore all existing forms of worship, ceremonies, churches, legal and moral codes will become superfluous. Instead of appearing as a force from without, God will now be within, and the unity of God and man will be fully accomplished. (Morton 37)

The Four Zoas depicts the transformation from the second to the third age, the sufferings that are inevitable for the historical Christ (Luvah) to be replaced by a truly Antinomian one, Los (or rather: the new integrity of Albion, with Los as *primus inter pares*, not excluding Urizen and Luvah, who had to come first in order that a higher integrity may be achieved). One slight alteration between the ages of Joachim of Flora and the phases presented in *The Four Zoas* needs to be pointed out. Although the Eternity from which the Zoas fell was indeed the age of the Father, Tharmas, it cannot easily be corresponded to the first age of the Everlasting Gospel, as it appears more idyllic than that. It seems that in

73

Blake's poem Eternity or original Innocence answers the Golden Age of myths, while Experience comprises both ordo conjugatorum and ordo clericorum.[122] While Joachim called the three periods the Ages of the Father, Son and the Holy Ghost, the Muggletonians (an English Joachite sect[123]) changed the denomination to the Ages of Water, Blood and Spirit which appear to be echoed in *The Four Zoas*, as the Age of Water is that of Tharmas, the Age of Blood is that of Urizen, initiator of bloody wars and – as the God of the Old Testament – of bloody revenges, as well as of Luvah, in whose robes of blood Jesus descended so that his blood can be spilled to prepare the way for the Age of the Spirit, presided over by Urthona-Los. Although in both Joachim of Flora's and Blake's writings ordo monachorum is depicted as the age of the greatest felicity and triumph it has to be pointed out that while Joachim's primary concern is with the advent of a new era in *society*, which then will comprise new spiritual men, *viri spiritualis,* in Blake's poems the accent is shifted and the main interest is in the birth of a *New Man* – who also embodies a new society.

We have previously pointed out that Luvah and Vala belong to the Szondian category of dual unionism and then demonstrated that Luvah represents the historical aspect of Christ. Once we accept these two theses, we can logically infer that Luvah's partner in the dual union is the Church. In the following passages we shall endeavour to substantiate this conclusion.

First and foremost it needs to be clarified that in Blake's poems two types of Church are presented: the Church Universal and the Church of Rome. The Church Universal is the only church Blake acknowledged as "it is composed of the Innocent <civilized> Heathen & the Uncivilized Savage who having not the Law do by nature the things contain in the Law" (*VLJ* 81). This church corresponds to the third age of the Everlasting Gospel, while the Church of Rome – with its adherence to the Ten Commandments and promulgation of conventional moral virtues – belongs to the second one.[124] The two are each other's opposite, as the basic tenet of the first is the Forgiveness of Sins while the second is based on the Punishment of Sins. Obviously, when we say that Luvah's partner in the dual union is the Church, we mean the Church of Rome.

Instead of citing the evident textual references to Vala as Church,[125] we shall concentrate on some contextual elements that prove their identity. Because of Blake's notion of the essential interconnectedness of the Church of Rome and the Old Testament, upon whose

---

[122] This observation is confirmed by the fact that Luvah and Urizen are inextricably bound in the poem.

[123] The sect flourished in the seventeenth century but survived in London until Blake's time.

[124] There has been a pungent debate as to whether or not in Joachim of Flora's third *status* the former laws shall be abrogated and the Church of Rome superseded (see Reeves passim); in Blake's poems – especially in *The Everlasting Gospel* – ordo monachorum as an age of Antinomian Christ/s.

Blake's objection to the Church of Rome is already formulated on plate 11 of *The Marriage of Heaven and Hell*:

... a system was formed, which some took advantage of & enslav'd the vulgar by attempting to realize or abstract the mental dieties from their objects: thus began Priesthood.

Choosing forms of worship from poetic tales.

And at length they pronounced that the Gods had orderd such things.

Thus men forgot that All deities reside in the human breast.

[125] In her fallen form she is referred to as "Rahab / Who is Mystery Babylon the Great the Mother of Harlots", who belongs to the "Synagogue of Satan", which "Clothed her with Scarlet robes & Gems / And on her forehead was her name written in blood" (*FZ* VIII, 106:329–330, 105:281–282), a straightforward allusion to Revelation 17:4–5 and 2:9.

doctrines he thought it was based, we would expect that Vala have strong links with Urizen (Old Testament God). And indeed, apart from a few brief encounters with Tharmas and Los, she is associated with Luvah and Urizen all through the poem. Vala's continuous conjunction with Urizen, her revengefulness, cruelty and militancy ("Rahab & Tirzah far different mantles prepare webs of torture / Mantles of despair girdles of bitter compunction shoes of indolence / Veils of ignorance covering from head to feet" /VIII, 113:218–220/) well corresponds to the idea of the false Church the best summary of which is given in *Jerusalem*:

> Man must & will have Some Religion; if he has not the Religion of Jesus, he will have the Religion of Satan, & will erect the Synagogue of Satan. calling the Prince of this World, God; and destroying all who do not worship Satan under the Name of God! . . . Every Religion that Preaches Vengeance for Sin is the Religion of the Enemy & Avenger; and not the Forgiver of Sin, and their God is Satan, Named by the Divine Name (52)

Vala assists Urizen in the demolition of all three aspects of Luvah, first by firing Urizen's furnaces, which melt her counterpart (II, 26–27), then by curbing Orc's rage which leads to the Demon's crucifixion on Urizen's Tree of Mystery (VII, 91 and VIII, 101[126]), and finally – as a member in the Synagogue of Satan – by voting for Jesus's death (VIII, 105). Revealingly, her role in the murdering of Christ is most emphatic when Luvah's Jesus-aspect is killed; she does not only vote for and then triumph over the crucifixion, but she herself slays him:

> But thou O Universal Humanity who is One Man blessed for Ever
> Recievest the Integuments woven Rahab beholds the Lamb of God
> She smites with her knife of flint *She destroys her own work*
> *Times after times* thinking to destroy the Lamb (VIII, 113:232–235 – emphasis added)

The physical aspect of Jesus, then, is the false Church's own projection, which she destroys time after time.

We can find further indications of Vala's intricate connection with Urizen in the fact that "[s]he spread herself thro all the branches" of the Tree of Mystery and "The Synagogue Created her from Fruit of Urizen's tree" (VIII, 101:85; 105:287). But just like Vala is born from Urizen, Urizen is also born from Vala; her seduction of Albion and giving life to Urizen can be seen as Blake's poetic rendering of the process, whereby the Church created a false conception of religion in Man. In the figure of Albion, the whole of mankind has fallen into Vala's trap:

> For nothing could restrain the dead in Beulah from descending
> Unto Ulros night tempted by the Shadowy females sweet
> Delusive cruelty they descend away from the Daughters of Beulah
> And Enter Urizens temple (VIII, 99:25–28)

---

[126] It is also interesting to note that when Orc is born, Vala takes charge over him, just like the Church appropriated Jesus (VII, 85:332).

Even Jerusalem cannot escape her influence (the most frequently applied adjective to describe Vala is 'delusive' and 'cruel') whom Rahab takes "A Willing Captive by delusive arts impelld / to Worship Urizens dragon form to offer her own Children / Upon the bloody Altar" (VIII, 111:598–600). Rahab's delusion then leads Jerusalem to weep over the dead body of Jesus (mistaking his garment for his essence) and to initiate the worship of death, the ultimate error in the teaching of the Church.

Finally, there remains one element that seems to bear special significance in our analysis. We know that Apocalypse starts immediately after the culmination of error. This climax in Urizen's case is the moment when he embraces the Shadowy Female, which is Blake saying that when false religion is completely absorbed by the false Church, the moment is ripe for the regeneration of both.

We have started our investigation of Luvah and Vala with a question: What could account for the apparent vagueness of the character of Luvah? After our analysis the following explanation suggests itself: because of the dual union between Luvah and Vala, the Zoa can only be examined together with his partner, with whom he is essentially one, as the historical Christ can only be understood when studied together with the Church of Rome, the two being inextricably bound.

CHAPTER IV

LOS AND ENITHARMON

For to be carnally minded is death
but to be spiritually minded is life and peace.
Rom. 8:6.

In the unfallen world Los had the name "Urthona", which may be a play on earth-owner (Bloom, *Blake's* 195). He then was the Ancient Man's sense of hearing ("Urthona was his name / In Eden; in the Auricular Nerves of Human life / Which is the Earth of Eden" [*FZ* I, 3–4:16–18]); the apocalyptic sense of music and poetry. His eternal name may also refer to his place in Blake's mapping proposal: Urthona – North subtly implying that he may be "the polestar of our moral being" (Bidney 110) as he is alluded to as the "immortal starry one"(*FZ* I, 3:14).

After the fall the Zoa takes the name Los, a name of as many possible implications as diverse the figure itself. 'Los' may refer to his own transition from Urthona to Los: the *loss* of original harmony. This is indeed the main concern of the poem: it describes "His fall into Division & his Resurrection to Unity / His fall into the Generation of Decay & Death & his Regeneration / by the Resurrection from the dead" (I, 4:20–22).

Another possible implication of the name – the most accepted among critics – appears to be as an anagram of '*Sol*', as he is frequently depicted as the forger of the sun/Sun. (Distinction has to be made between the material sun and the spiritual one, which latter is the human imagination. In the Lambeth books Los's sun seems to be the material sun while in the major prophecies the light emanating from Los is the visionary, apocalyptic light of imagination; he is Son/Sun and Los/Logos.)

Somewhat different from the first two readings of the name is Harold Bloom's proposal, according to which 'Los'may be derived from the Chaucerian "loos", a word for poetic fame (Commentary in Blake 907).

Finally, the Los = soul hypothesis may also be vindicated as in the body-soul dichotomy of the Ancient Man Los undoubtedly stands for the latter.

The etymology of the name of Los's emanation, Enitharmon – as the derivation from Enion and Tharmas – has already been touched upon. Kathleen Raine's suggestion that it may read "in harmony" [with Los] (*Blake* 2: 139) does not appear to be quite justifiable inasmuch as in their fallen state Los and Enitharmon are just as incongruous as any other couple, while in their eternal form their unity is just as – and no more – harmonious than that of the other three Zoas.

More convincing is Foster Damon's intimation, which finds the name a derivation from the Greek *(z)enith* plus *(h)armon(y)* (*A Blake* 457)[127]; an etymology that accounts for the close connections between fallen Enitharmon and Urizen, whose realm is the Zenith (*FZ* I, 18:495).

---

[127] His other reading of the name as a derivation from the Greek *anarithmon* ('numberless') is somewhat difficult to explain; most probably a reference to her early appearance as Eternal Female, or Great Mother (in *MHH* and *Europe*).

The first brief mention of Enitharmon and Urthona is in *The Marriage of Heaven and Hell*, where Enitharmon – not yet the Emanation of Los – is the Eternal Female bringing forth the revolutionary boy, later to be called Orc. Urthona is even less specific; we learn that the jealous king, nascent Urizen, is buried in the ruins on Urthona's dens. Apart from two passing references to him in *America*, and one in *Europe*, Urthona disappears from Blake's poetry to come back only in *The Four Zoas*.

Enitharmon is first mentioned by the name in *Europe*. The poem foreshadows Enitharmon's later role as Female Will and depicts her as teaching Mankind the false religion of chastity:

> Go! tell the human race that Womans love is Sin!
> That an Eternal life awaits the worms of sixty winters
> In an allegorical abode where existence hath never come:
> Forbid all Joy, & from her childhood shall the little female
> Spread nets in every secret path. (Plate 5)

Los, too, appears first in *Europe* as Enitharmon's spouse but is withdrawn immediately, leaving Enitharmon to establish her rule uncontrolled. He returns at the end of the poem calling his sons to the strife of blood, the French Revolution.

It is in *The Book of Urizen* that the outlines of Los, the Eternal Prophet are beginning to show. Urizen, rent from Los's side attempts to set himself up as omnipotent god. He breaks away from the Eternals, unorganized. Los, commissioned to watch over Urizen, forges him a physical body which goes hand in hand with the creation of Time. Terrified at the image of his own making, the bound Urizen, pity divides Los's soul; he himself falls. Simultaneously, Enitharmon, the first separate female figure is born, upon whom he begets Orc and binds him down with the Chain of Jealousy.

The Book of Los retells the binding of Urizen resulting in Los's fall, as well as depicts the creation of the material sun, a theme adumbrated in *The Book of Ahania*.

We have now arrived at *The Four Zoas*, which discusses Urthona in more detail; albeit the "data which Blake has left for a full account of Urthona, the eternal form of Los, cannot be called an embarrassment of riches" (Frye, *Fearful* 291). He is the only Zoa who never manifests in his own person, but always appears in his fallen form, which is divided fourfold: Los, Enitharmon, the Spectre and the Shadow. No wonder that in the poem this most elusive character is called "dark Urthona" thirteen times.

In the first night we learn that Los and Enitharmon are born from fallen Tharmas and Enion. (The circumstances of their birth/the story of the disruption of the unity of Urthona is suppressed and recast only in Nights IV and VII.) With Los and Enitharmon the concept of Time and Space is born into this world: "He could control the times & seasons, & the days & years / She could control the spaces, regions, desart, flood & forest" (I, 9:241–242). From the moment of their birth, these children are as haughty and self-absorbed as humble and selfless are their parents. Enitharmon shows traces of those hypocritical ideas that are later to be elaborated as Female Will:

> To make us happy let them weary their immortal powers
> While we draw in their sweet delights while we return them scorn
> On scorn to feed our discontent; for if we grateful prove
> They will withhold sweet love, whose food is thorns & bitter roots. (I, 10:254–256)

The relationship between Los and Enitharmon is dominated by suspicion; Los feels alternate love and hate, Enitharmon scorn and jealousy, as a couple they are sullen and self-destructive.[128]

Los's obsessive pursuit of his sister-spouse during the first night is met by contempt and scorn; Enitharmon at this stage is "La Belle Dame Sans Merci . . . she is the feminine agent of male sexual humiliation, who is herself governed by *ennui*" (Ostriker 159). In their constant fights Enitharmon is assisted by Urizen.

Offhand, one would think that of all the characters in the poem she is the least likely to contribute to the amelioration of Albion's plight. However destructive she may seem in the first night, there are subtle hints to her future role in the regeneration of Albion. Enitharmon is likened to a bright rainbow (daughter to Thaumas, as has previously been pointed out), a motif which implies the promise of a new covenant between God and His people. For the Romantic artist, Ágnes Péter explains, the rainbow does not simply mean particles of light in a mathematically construed space, but it also signifies individual experiences, memories and associations as well as emotions; in short, things that are not describable in generic terms (Péter 6).

Furthermore, as a result of her (temporary) union with Los, Enitharmon gives birth to Orc, who shall later – albeit indirectly (through his death) – trigger off the Apocalypse. It is not accidental that of all the Zoas and Emanations, Los and Enitharmon are the only ones to be portrayed as a couple *as well as* brother and sister. Their incestuous relationship may have traces in alchemy, in which, on the ground that brother and sister were of a common genetic source, their incestuous union represented the chemical wedding of the opposites, the *mysterious coniunctionis,* which led to a new alchemical birth, metaphoric of spiritual regeneration. From this wedding the Philosopher's Stone was born, which in Christian alchemy was held to correspond with Christ, "the Messiah of Nature, who had the apocalyptic function of restoring both fallen and divided man and the fallen and fragmented universe to the perfection of their original unity" (Abrams 160).[129] In *The Four Zoas* the incestuous embrace of Los and Enitharmon leads to the birth of Orc, Blake's equivocal Christ.

It is also Enitharmon – even if unconsciously, indeed much against her wish – who shelters Jerusalem (after she is expelled from Tharmas's bosom), the saving remnant of Eternity.

> Three gates within Glorious & bright open into Beulah
> From Enitharmons inward parts but the bright female terror
> Refusd to open the bright gates she closd and barrd them fast
> Lest Los should enter into Beulah thro her beautiful gates

---

[128] Judith Lee suggests that it is possible that to some extent the Los–Enitharmon relationship, central to *The Four Zoas,* was modelled after the Orlando-Angelica story at the centre of Ludovico Ariosto's *Orlando Furioso.* "The fictional worlds of both poems are mindscapes in which continual change reflects the imperfect perceptions of its characters, and in both human folly is represented by the lure of a disdainful, beautiful woman. . . . Angelica's paradoxical nature generates the central ironic tension in the Furioso – between illusion and reality; Enitharmon's disdain for and fear of Los generates the central tension in *Vala* – between dominance and reciprocity" (36–38).

[129] It must be noted here that Blake – like to his Romantic contemporaries – had a teleological view of history, in which the final state of integrity is higher than the original, primordial unity.

The Emanation stood before the Gates of Enitharmon
Weeping. the Daughters of Beulah silent in the Porches
Spread her a couch unknown to Enitharmon here reposd
Jerusalem (I, 20:563–570)

Night II shows Los and Enitharmon at their nadir; they are extracting a sadistic pleasure from the sorrow of Urizen and the woes of Vala and Luvah and are determined to plant division into the soul of Urizen and Ahania. It is interesting to note here that while their parents, Enion and Tharmas were introduced to the poem as adults, their behaviour was/ is more childlike than that of their offsprings, who are so uncannily adultlike in their actions.[130] They accuse each other of infidelity and in their contentions we hear the echo of their parents' battle. In Enitharmon's sinister soliloquy the Female Will gets its full expression: "The joy of woman is the Death of her most best beloved / Who dies for Love of her / In torments of fierce jealousy & pangs of adoration" (34:350–352). This is exactly what she wants to achieve when she – only a few lines later! – deludes Los (with a song ironically resembling the Song of Solomon), kindling false hope in him:

O I am weary lay thine hand upon me or I faint
I faint beneath these beams of thine
For thou hast touchd my five senses & they answerd thee
Now I am nothing & I sink
And on the bed of silence sleep till thou awakest me (34:374–378)

There is a perplexing point that needs to be mentioned here. All through Night II everything indicates that Los and Enitharmon are fallen from Eternity; their sadistic joy at their fellow Zoas' sufferings, Enitharmon's hypocricy and the very name Los bears (Los is the fallen manifestation of the eternal Urthona, as has been pointed out previously). And yet, at one point the text disrupts our expectation and tells us that

Los and Enitharmon walkd forth on the dewy Earth
Contracting or expanding their all flexible senses
At will to murmur in the flowers small as the honey bee
At will to stretch across the heavens & step from star to star
. . . .
While round their heads the Elemental Gods kept harmony (34:295–301)

clearly implying that even in their fallen form they have retained some of their eternal potentials and that they might provide a link between the Eternals and the disintegrated members of Albion. The reader is left some time to ponder about these enigmatic lines as the escalating conflict is temporarily halted and Los and Enitharmon are withdrawn from the following night.

---

[130] This seems to be in keeping with Jeanne-Pierre van Meerbeek's hypothesis according to which there is a correspondance between Piaget's four stages of psychological development and Szondi's four drive vectors; the first – most simple – stage, the Sensorimotor Stage answering the Contact drive, congruous with Tharmas while the fourth – the most complex – stage, the Formal Operations Stage corresponding to the Ego drive, which is parallel with Los. For the Piaget–Szondi correlations see Van Meerbeek 185–190.

The main agent of the central nights is Los, the main pattern is incarnation. Tharmas commissions his son to rebuild the ruined world of Urizen, a request that Los indignantly defies, refusing to accept Tharmas's supremacy. Instead, unexpectedly reversing his earlier enmity towards Urizen, he – supported by Enitharmon – hails him as God.[131] Tharmas retorts for this inobediance by tearing Enitharmon apart from Los and by this deed he gives birth to a most enigmatic character: the Spectre of Urthona. Aided and protected by the Spectre, Los is compelled to bind the fallen Urizen lest he should rise again. The reward for this arduous task is the reunion with Enitharmon. "In binding Urizen, Los retakes lost ground; in reclaiming Enitharmon, however, he accomplishes something even more crucial; he begins to reestablish his authentic role and identity"(Wilkie and Johnson 93). But he is not yet ripe for this reunion. Before his regeneration may take place he has to go through the totality of Experience and fall further away from his original station. As Night IV closes and the incarnation of Urizen is complete, Los "terrifid at the shapes / Enslavd humanity put on he became what he beheld / He became what he was doing he was himself transformd" (55:285–287) becoming Urizenic.

The central event of Night the Fifth is the birth of Orc from the now fallen Los and Enitharmon. Los is depicted here at his worst. His affinity with Urizen at this point gets an eloquent expression as we see him binding down his own son. Just as Urizen cast Luvah into the furnaces of affliction (implying the suppression of energy) in Night the Second now that Urizen is mentally destructed, Los takes over his job and chains down the new incarnation of Luvah: Orc.

What was suppressed in the more cryptic *The Book of Urizen* is made explicit here: The reason Los nails down his son with the Chain of Jealousy growing from his bosom is that "now he feard Eternal Death & uttermost Extinction" (60:75). Los's expression of anguish and fear is immediately followed by the channeling of his aggression and frustration into the building of Golgonooza, city of art, a supreme example of what later came to be termed as sublimation.[132]

With the chaining of Orc Los establishes the "Orc Cycle", depicted so concisely in *The Mental Traveller,* a process whereby the Promethean youth ages into Urizen, a transformation paradoxically leading to Apocalypse. The Chain of Jealousy becomes swift vegetation sustained by Orc's life; Los repents too late, in vain are all his efforts to free his son. Enitharmon's pain triggers a process of regeneration, as the so-far arrogant and cruel energies of Los and Enitharmon are now chanelled through suffering. As the seed of sympathy appears they no longer strive to extract cruel delight of their fellow Zoas' plight,

---

[131] Wilkie and Johnson find this sudden change in Los's attitude toward Urizen "understandable when we remember that this oath of allegiance is not a fully considered act but in part a startled reaction to instinct's demand to total power. . . . Art wishes to owe nothing to anyone; for its own purpose it may spurn one pretender by seeming to shift allegiance to another – but only for as long as it is necessary to alter the balance of power" (87).

[132] Brenda Webster understands the building of Golgonooza quite differently: "When his son is still too young to be a menace, Los attempts to forestall Oedipal conflict by building Golgonooza around Enitharmon to hide her. Golgonooza's inclusion of a symbolic replica of the female organs, Luban's gates, suggests that the city of art, although developing from a wish for exclusive possession of the mother's body, eventually re-creates that body in a form that is under the creator's control" (*Blake's Prophetic* 230).

It is interesting to note here, that in Blake's engraving of the scene – mother and Orc embracing with the father looking at his son – Los is portrayed bearded, decrepit and exhausted unlike in any other pictures which show him young and vigorous.

Picture 4 The First Book of Urizen (1794)

on the contrary, they begin to intimate that the Zoas are essentially connected and the pain of the one inevitably effects all the others.

> When satiated with grief they returnd back to Golgonooza
> Enitharmon on the road of Dranthon felt the inmost gate
> Of her bright heart burst open & again close with a deadly pain
> Within her heart Vala began to reanimate in bursting sobs
> And when the Gate was open she beheld that dreary Deep
> Where bright Ahania wept. She also saw the infernal roots
> Of the chain of Jealousy & felt the rendings of fierce howling Orc (63:176–182)

From Night the Sixth Enitharmon and Los are completely withdrawn; we only get a glimpse of their barren and doleful world through which Urizen travels to meet the chained Orc. Lest this encounter should take place, the Spectre and Tharmas ally against Urizen to defend Orc. The alliance can be read as a step towards regeneration as this is the first positive turn in the poem's action. Even though the Spectre and Tharmas have been allied before, then – in Night the Fourth – they joined forces *against* Los, while now they strive together *in defence of* Orc. "The birth of Orc is the first appearance of Luvah in the postlapsarian world. With his appearance, all the Zoas are present again, though each is self-divided and flawed. However dimly, the Spectre of Urthona and Tharmas now long for apocalypse, and instinctively they associate Orc with that hope" (Commentary in Blake 958).

Of all the nights, Night the Seventh has given rise to most polemics, conceptual as well as philological.[133] The night is crucial as this is the night of long-awaited imaginative awakening. This notion is intimated by the upward movement of the scenes depicted; in the first passages we see Urizen descending into the Caves of Orc (Urizen and Orc defying each other) while the night ends with Los "springing up aloft / Into the heavens of Enitharmon" (90:464–465) where he lovingly embraces Urizen, his long-contempted arch-enemy.

It shall now be examined how the poem proceeds from an apparent stalemate to the presage of the apocalypse. The night begins with a deep psychic conflict, Urizen facing Orc. Their strife comes to a mental deadlock – the last phase of the Orc-cycle – with Orc transforming into a Urizenic character. Apparently initiation starts elsewhere; it "involves the discovery or activation of unsuspected imaginative powers"(Bidney 142). As Tharmas is still the raging turbulence desperately seeking Enion, the only Zoa left to hold out the hope of awakening is Urthona.

Urthona here is depicted as three different characters: Los, the Spectre and (the Shadow of) Enitharmon. This splitting up of the primal unity remains as long as they conceive themselves as distinct creatures. But some traces of coming to consciousness can already be discerned in the lament of Los, who now realizes that he has been completely separated from his Emanation:

Los saw her stretchd the image of death upon his witherd valleys
Her Shadow went forth & returnd Now she was pale as Snow
When the mountains & hills are coverd over & the paths of Men shut up
But when her spirit returnd as ruddy as a morning when
The ripe fruit blushes into joy in heavens eternal halls
Sorrow shot thro him from his feet it shot up to his head
. . . .
Then Los mournd on the dismal wind in his jealous lamentation
Why can I not Enjoy thy beauty Lovely Enitharmon
When I return from clouds of Grief in the wandring Elements
Where thou in thrilling joy in beaming summer loveliness
Delectable reposest ruddy in my absence flaming with beauty
Cold pale in sorrow at my approach trembling at my terrific
Forehead & eyes thy lips decay like roses in the spring
How art thou Shrunk thy grapes that burst in summers vast Excess

---

[133] Of the latter see Textual Notes in Blake 836 and Donald Ault, *Re-visioning* 105–140. See *Appendix IV–VI.*

> Shut up in little purple covering faintly bud & die
>
> ·
>
> All things beside the woful Los enjoy the delights of beauty
> Once how I sang & calld the beasts & birds to their delights
> Nor knew that I alone exempted from the joys of love
> Must war with secret monsters of the animating worlds (81–82:172–201)

Enitharmon, too, has some recollection of the Golden Age and the disruption of the unity but her recollections are rather sketchy "forgetfulness quite wrapd me up" (83:260) and her aim is still somewhat negative: to punish Vala. It seems that both Los and Enitharmon are still to mature through suffering before they may take the first conscious step towards regeneration.

It is nothing short of startling to note that of all the three manifestations of Urthona in the fallen world it is the Spectre who retains the closest link with Eternity. He can recall moments that escaped Enitharmon unremembered and strives to restore the primal unity:

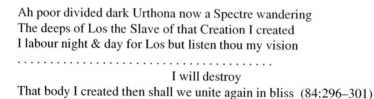

> Ah poor divided dark Urthona now a Spectre wandering
> The deeps of Los the Slave of that Creation I created
> I labour night & day for Los but listen thou my vision
>
> ·
>   I will destroy
> That body I created then shall we unite again in bliss (84:296–301)

The Spectre is yet to be followed by Los and Enitharmon in his craving for regeneration. The redeeming pain or the culmination of error that finally changes the latter two into prime agents of the apocalyptic process is the traumatic birth of Vala from Enitharmon's heart: "Los wept his fierce soul was terrifid / At the shrieks of Enitharmon at her tossings nor could his eyes percieve / The cause of her dire anguish for she lay the image of Death" (85:318–320).

From this moment imaginative initiation may commence. Initiation – albeit traditionally associated with Los – is itself threefold, corresponding to the three distinct manifestations of the disintegrated Zoa. The insights the characters gain may be called *psychological*, *moral* and *ontological* in their primary emphasis.[134]

The first initiation is *psychological* and is connected to the Spectre. The Spectre teaches that in order that Los may unite with his Emanation he first has to accept his so-far repressed, monstrous energies as his real self. The ancient harmony between imagination and his creative potential cannot be recovered until "Thou art united with thy Spectre Consummating by pains & labours / That mortal body & by Self annihilation back returning / To Life Eternal" (85:342–344). It is an impressive fact that of all the characters that inhabit Albion's beleaguered brain this most deformed Spectre shows the deepest psychological insight.[135] He is the one to realize that "if we unite in one another better

---

[134] My understanding of these genuinely complex passages has been informed by Bidney 139–156.

[135] In accord with the findings of psychoanalysis – and indeed with the tradition of Platonism – the Spectre teaches that in order that one may recover one has to "Unbar the Gates of Memory" and accept what one finds "Not as another but as thy real Self" (VII 85:346, 347).

world will be / Opend within your heart & loins & wondrous brain" (85:353–354), clearly reflecting that he not only apprehends the urgency of the restoration of Urthona but also intimates the essential interconnectedness of all the Zoas and that this union shall bring about the redemption of his fellow Zoas, that of Luvah-heart, Tharmas-loins and Urizen-wondrous brain.

Yet the psychological awakening, the embrace of the Spectre – though indispensable – is not in itself sufficient for the regeneration of Albion. More modes of initiation must follow.

The second mode of awakening is *moral* and is associated with Los. It involves the quelling of the ego and the voluntary renunciation of one's selfhood. Los's loving embrace of his Spectre is all the more respectable as the Spectre rewards his impulse of forgiveness and affection with rebuking him for his past sins. Los – though furious – shows examplary self-surrender:

> Spectre horrible thy words astound my Ear
> With irresistible conviction I feel I am not one of those
> Who when convincd can still persist. tho furious.controllable
> By Reasons power.
> . . . .
> Come then into my Bosom & in thy shadowy arms bring with thee
> My lovely Enitharmon. I will quell my fury & teach
> Peace to the Soul of dark revenge & repentance to Cruelty (86:361–369)

The union of Spectre and Los, a crucial part in the poem, has given rise to a number of arguments as to its genuineness. Some claim that the merger is unaccounted for and consider this apparently arbitrary triumph of love and forgiveness as a structural and/or psychological weakness of the poem as they feel that Blake does not anatomize the moment of relief simply focuses on the new perspectives. Wilkie and Johnson, on the other hand, compare the poem to (other) Romantic masterpieces *(Prometheus Unbound* and *The Prelude)* and argue that far from being a flaw in the poem, this gap is a real masterstroke as it shows Blake's acumen: "If the conversion were totally explainable, the training of the psychiatrists could be much abbreviated and all mental illness, perhaps even all social problems related to it, could be cured in one and the same way. Blake's wisdom in leaving this hiatus of explanation is confirmed in other great works that explore the spiritual dark night and recovery from it" (159).

Los's self-transcendence is consummated in Mental fires. The age-old metaphor of cleansing fire implies that Los's past sins are purged away. There is however one past deed that Los has yet to remedy. His atonement involves Enitharmon and the third mode of initiation: the *ontological* awakening. This final insight is the most complex of all as it includes, as well as is dependent upon, the other two.

We have seen how – in the Fifth Night – Los chained down his son exposing Orc to Promethean sufferings. We would expect that before the final step in the regeneration of Urthona may take place this cruel deed be counteracted. The final lesson that Los has to learn is that – in conjunction with Enitharmon/*anarithmon*/the Great Mother – his task is lifegiving. This ontological insight, the "initiation into creative Becoming" (Bidney 151) Los feels highly compelling; "Stern desire / I feel to fabricate embodied semblances in which the dead / May live" (90:439–441). He is assisted in his work by Enitharmon as

Los "drew a line upon the walls of shining heaven / And Enitharmon tincturd it with beams of blushing love" (90:466–467). All the past errors of this Zoa of Imagination are carefully undone so that Los may deserve the intimation in his character of the fourth one of Daniel 3:25. Willingly accepting his Spectre and overcoming his own fear of his offsprings, Los now lovingly creates new life and thus fulfills all three modes of initiation necessary for the imaginative awakening of Night the Seventh.

> Los loved them & refusd to Sacrifice their infant limbs
> And Enitharmons smiles & tears prevaild over self protection
> They rather chose to meet Eternal death than to destroy
> The offspring of their Care & Pity Urthonas spectre was comforted (90:482–485)

With all the manifestations of his fallen existence recovered, Urthona – the last Zoa to disintegrate – is restored first.[136] The low image density of these segments of the night points to the relative importance of these passages in the whole poem.[137]

Night the Eighth continues to depict Los and Enitharmon as compassionate workers for salvation who create vegetative bodies to the Spectres. The destructive furnaces of affliction have now given way to the creative furnaces of Los:

> In Golgonooza Los's anvils stand & his Furnaces rage
> Ten thousand demons labour at the forges Creating Continually
> The times & spaces of Mortal Life the Sun the Moon the Stars
> In periods of Pulsative furor beating into wedges & bars
> Then drawing into wires the terrific Passions & Affections
> Of Spectrous dead. Thence to the Looms of Catherdron conveyd
> The Daughters of Enitharmon weave the ovarium & the integument
> In soft silk drawn from their own bowels in lascivious delight
> With songs of sweet cadence to the turning spindle & reel
> Lulling the weeping spectres of the dead. Clothing their limbs
> With gifts & gold of Eden. Astonishd stupified with delight
> The terrors put on their sweet clothing on the banks of Arnon
> Whence they plunge into the river of space for a period till
> The dread Sleep of Ulro is past. (113:202–215)

Los's labours are counteracted by Urizen's warlike preparations whose engines of deceit, hooks, screws and harsh instruments "to grate the soul into destruction" (102:136) are in striking contrast with the redeeming actions of his adversary. Gradually we feel that the moment is ripe for the clash along the North-South axis of Creativity between Los and Urizen. The figure of Urizen here (as well as the forces associated with him) integrate a

---

[136] We know from the previous chapter that the reunion of Urthona is followed by the reintegration of Luvah and Vala. As Urthona is parallel with the Ego drive and Luvah with the Sexual drive, Szondi's note that the reunification of the opposing factors [Zoa and Emanation] of the Ego and Sexual drives is of primary importance as their disintegration effect more the disintegration of the whole of the personality than the division within the Paroxysmal and Contact drives (*Módszertan* 216), shows a striking allegiance to the ideas formulated in *The Four Zoas*.

[137] For a discussion of related matters see Ide, *Image Patterns*.

critique of contemporary religious, political and social ideas. Los, on the other hand, "Contemplated inspird by the holy Spirit / Los builds the Walls of Golgonooza against the stirring battle" (101:108–109). As is appropriate to the Zoa of Imagination, he builds the city of Art – Golgonooza, a Golgotha of Nous and Zoa, a Calvary of Mind and Body (Fogel 229)[138] – using creative art as a main means of repulsing and counterbalancing Urizen's advance. However, as Leopold Damrosch so aptly notes: "Golgonooza represents the best that can be done with physical materials – with 'material' materials – but in using them at all it confesses its distance from Eden" (quoted in Peterfreund 122).

Coming from the above it is interesting to note that even though the regeneration of Urthona has apparently taken place he continues to be depicted as Los, a fact that indicates that the restoration of the Zoa of Imagination at the end of the previous night cannot have been complete. Though his disintegrated parts have been united we have to bear in mind that Urthona is a member of a higher entelechy; he is one of the Quaternals making up the Ancient Man. The only way he can reassume his ancient bliss is to reintegrate into the Universal Brotherhood of Eden, without which "a Perfect Unity / Cannot Exist" (I, 3:4–5) as "Rent from Eternal Brotherhood we die & are no more" (III, 41:75). This explanation is further substantiated by the fact that whenever he is referred to as Urthona in the course of Night the Eighth he is depicted in the context of his fellow Zoas (107:466–469; 476–479). Urthona then can only be fully restored when the fellow Quaternals have been reunited with their emanations (or at least show some signs of coming to consciousness).

The beginning of the final night eloquently proves that Los's spiritual regeneration is not yet complete. In the prelude to the Apocalypse the Luvah-Urizen conflict has reached its climax; with the crucifixion of Jesus in Luvah's robes of blood the final manifestation of Luvah seems to be subdued.

> And Los & Enitharmon builded Jerusalem weeping
> Over the Sepulcher & over the Crucified body
> Which to their Phantom Eyes appear'd still in the Sepulcher
> But Jesus stood beside them in the Spirit Separating
> Their Spirit from their body. Terrified at Non Existence
> For such they deemd the death of the body. (IX, 117:1–6)

Los does not seem to be aware of the significance of Jesus's descent and mistakenly identifies the death of the vegetated body with total annihilation. Paradoxically, this misapprehension urges him to start the Apocalypse, as he can no longer control his prophetic rage and tears down the Sun and the Moon "cracking the heavens across from immense to immense" (117:9). Such an instinctual impulse, however, cannot in itself restore the Ancient Man; redemption will be achieved through the instrumentality of all four Zoas. With the process of universal regeneration started, the Shadow of Enitharmon and the Spectre of Urthona fade away, as two shadows mingling on a wall, to be finally buried in the ruins of the collapsing universe.

---

[138] Fogel's interpretation of the etymology of Golgonooza as Calvary of Mind and Body is justified by Daniel Albright's assertion (originally formulated to describe Yeats's poetry but fully applicable to Blake as well): "One of the great themes in all poetry written since Keats is the construction of an art-world designed to satisfy the human desire for perpetual joy – and the subsequent discovery that a paradise will turn cold and sterile unless it contains human pain . . . as well" (54).

In *The Four Zoas* the fully imaginative life as typified in art has set mankind on the road to fulfilment. But after art has done its work it recedes. ... It is an impressive fact that after Los takes the initiative early in Night IX by tearing down the universe, he is given almost no role in the remainder of the poem. In the final lines Blake writes almost jubilantly that the "Spectre of Prophecy" and the "Spectre of Los" have departed. ... It probably means ... that art itself must avoid setting itself up as a God. ... We may feel a pang of disappointment at the departure of Los as a dramatic character, though his role is fulfilled and though we know that his primal self Urthona lives and he is back at his important work. But in Eternity, when Urthona is restored to his ancient strength, his function is to make the weaponry for intellectual warfare, not to fight these wars himself. The effect of the conclusion is to reduce the stature of the artist as such in order to place all persons, humanity, humankind at the acme of reality. (Wilkie and Johnson 236–237)

The discussion of Urthona-Los has shown that he is much more heterogeneous a figure than would be expected from the minor prophecies. The question presents itself with special urgency: What makes the character of Urthona-Los in *The Four Zoas* so genuinely complex that even Northrop Frye acknowledges that some of his interpretations of the Zoa are tentative (*Fearful* 291). We have seen in the previous chapter how the fact that Luvah is depicted as having three different manifestations presents special difficulties in conceptualizing his character. We have also found that Luvah's lack of definition is partly due to his intricate bonds with Urizen. We face similar problems in the case of Urthona. He, too, is depicted as three (sometimes even as four) characters, but while Luvah's different manifestations succeed one another, all the three members of Urthona are simultaneously present in the poem. And just as Luvah, Los too has a complementary character; a projection of his own self: the Spectre.

The Spectre of Urthona, probably Blake's most original invention, has been interpreted all too differently as the rational power in man (Damon, *A Blake* 341), man's anciently repressed energy (Bidney 99) or the fearful ego or selfhood of fallen man (Bloom, *A Blake* 229–230).[139] His elusiveness is clearly seen in the fact that even Frye – who is considered to have given the best commentary on the character – appears to attempt to escape anomalies by recourse to exterior sources. Indeed he asserts that "the conception of the Spectre of Urthona seems to have broken on Blake quite suddenly. . . . Eventually it burst the whole Zoa scheme altogether, and was one of the chief reasons for abandoning the poem" (*Fearful* 298).[140]

---

[139] Robert Hume suggests that the spectre is the reverse or negative side of the male component and "is, or related to, the opposite Zoa. . . . This is logical: the spectre consists of undeveloped functions, which will plainly be those which are opposite or opposed to the dominant functions in the individual" (250). As in Hume's interpretation of Blake's Quaternity Los is opposed to Tharmas we would expect that the Spectre of Urthona be Tharmic, an expectation not substantiated by the poem.

"Each man's Spectre of Urthona is that part in him that begins by fearing old age, poverty, sickness, loneliness, and then expands to an omnipresent anxiety, a nameless dread of death-in-life, of time as an oppressive burden increasing in weight" (Commentary by H. Bloom in Blake 955).

[140] Frye concludes that the Spectre is clock-time, it is "the isolated subjective aspect of existence in this world, the energy with which man or any other living thing copes with nature. . . . One might call Blake's Spectre of Urthona the will" (*Fearful* 292).

The best example of the complexity of the Spectre is to be found in his extremely problematic appearance at the end of Night the Sixths:

> Round his loins a girdle glowd with many colourd fires
> In his hand a knotted Club whose knots like mountains frownd
> Desart among the Stars them withering with its ridges cold
> Black scales of iron arm the dread visage iron spikes instead
> Of hair shoot from his orbed skull. his glowing eyes
> Burn like two furnaces. he calld with Voice of Thunder. (75:303–308)

The perplexing description makes it rather difficult to visualize this peculiar character but there is much more to it than just Blake's effort to make the poem even more obscure (fulfilling his own admonition that the thing which could be "made Explicit to the Idiot" was not worth his care [*Letter to Dr Trusler* 23 August, 1799]). What is remarkable about the Spectre is that he mingles characteristics of all the main (male) figures in the poem thus emphasizing their interrelatedness. The girdle round the Spectre's loins may be the same tightening girdle as grew around *Los*'s bosom in the previous night turning eventually into the Chain of Jealousy. The description of his knotted Club is reminiscent of the imagery used to depict *Urizen*'s journey through the devastated universe, just as the Spectre's voice of thunder is reverberated in Urizen's voice of inarticulate thunder. (The black scales may also be interpreted as subtly recalling the building of the Mundane Shell by Urizen, when "the Sons of Urizen / With compasses divide the deep; they the strong scales erect" [II, 28:141–142].) The cold ridges are those of *Tharmas*'s ridgy waves that surround him whenever he appears in his fallen form. The iron spikes instead of hair compare to the sparks issuing from Los's hair when exasperated he clashes with Tharmas in Night the Fourth. The Spectre's orbed skull echoes *Luvah*'s orb of blood of the first night, just like the glowing eyes that burn like furnaces recall the chained *Orc*.

Why is the Spectre's physical appearance so meticulously described and why the unmistakable parallels between him and all the Zoas? We may hope to find an answer to this question in Szondi. The *Category of "Lost Genius" and "Patricide"* of the Ego drive shows close affinities with Los. As Szondi's descriptions apply to the fallen aspects of the Zoas we shall look for parallels in Night the Fifth as that is the night when Los's fall is completed. (No longer in conscious communication with Eternity "Their senses unexpansive in one steadfast bulk remain" [57:19].) We recall how the now-Urizenic Los bound his son with the Chain of Jealousy, an apt example of the pathologic jealousy of the members in Szondi's category. "There is always one family member whom they suspect of intentionally interfering with the free development of their genius and who then becomes the object of hatred and death wishes" (Szondi, *Experimental* 190). This consuming hatred finds expression in fits of murderous rage and aggression; it is in one such fit – when he can no longer curb his fear of Orc – that Los (with the help of the Spectre) chains down his son.

> Grief rose upon his ruddy brows. a tightening girdle grew
> Around his bosom like a bloody cord. in secret sobs
> He burst it, but next morn another girdle succeeds
> Around his bosom. Every day he viewd the fiery youth
> With silent fear & his immortal cheeks grew deadly pale

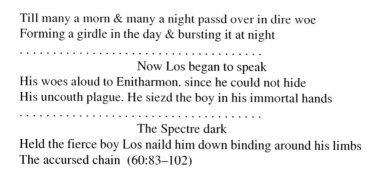

> Till many a morn & many a night passd over in dire woe
> Forming a girdle in the day & bursting it at night
> . . . .
> Now Los began to speak
> His woes aloud to Enitharmon. since he could not hide
> His uncouth plague. He siezd the boy in his immortal hands
> . . . .
> The Spectre dark
> Held the fierce boy Los naild him down binding around his limbs
> The accursed chain (60:83–102)

For all their obsessive suspicion and jealousy, some may later "return with great love and affection to the once hated partner" (Szondi, *Experimental* 190), just like Los soon repents having chained Orc and intends to unbind him "Even if his own death resulted so much pity him paind" (62:154).

We have so far attempted to justify our claim that the portrayal of Los discloses a lot of similarities with the Category of "Lost Genius" and "Patricide" of the Ego drive. His association with the Ego drive is further supported by the fact that Szondi intimated that this drive – unlike the other three – is a *specifically human* drive and without the Ego drive man would live the life of a selfless, unconscious animal (Szondi, *Módszertan* 250). As in Blake's poems Los is the artist and art is an exclusively human phenomenon, the Los = Ego assumption seems vindicated.

In the light of the above we may now try to find an answer to the question concerning the Spectre, a complementary character to Los. The inclusion of the different characteristics of all the Zoas into his figure seems to be explained by the fact that he is the ego of the personality. "The ego is the bridge which is capable of spanning all the antithetical poles of the psyche. The ego is the complex, manifold axis of that wheel of fate upon whose poles the psychic antithetic pairs are attached" (Szondi–Moser–Webb 267), it is the *pontifex oppositorum* of the personality (Szondi, *Ember* 20; Lukács, *Szondi* 36–37). The Los/ Spectre = ego/bridge hypothesis is substantiated by the fact that Los is the first one to regenerate and the redemption of the others Zoas seems to be conditional upon his resurrection.

The diverse explanations as to the Spectre's identity may be understood if we apprehend that the ego is not to be associated with an unequivocal place in psychic events. "On the contrary, the ego appears to move on various axes, for example from the conscious to the unconscious, from subject to object, from the drive sphere to the external world. In other words, the ego is dynamic in a double sense: first it alters its position within the psyche, and, second, it is itself transformed through its continual pursuit of other functions" (Szondi–Moser–Webb 39), just like Los gets further and further removed from his original place in the psyche and is gradually transformed as a result of his interactions with his fellow Zoas.

We have seen that in order that Los might start the Apocalypse he (as well as the Spectre and Enitharmon) had to attain three types of insight: psychological, moral and ontological. Similarly, the condition precedent to an efficiently functioning ego is that it must be capable of

1. Transcendence; hence, the ability to cross from one area to another
2. Integration; that is, the capacity to reconstruct a whole from its complementary parts
3. Participation; hence, the ability again to attain a state of unity (*Wieder-eins-Sein-Können*) to possess a portion of another one, whether that one is person or thing, world or universe. (Szondi–Moser–Webb 268)

Integration is close to psychological initiation, the acceptance and reintegration of the Spectre; transcendence is similar to moral insight in that Los has to annihilate his previous self in order to transcend it; and finally participation is analogous with ontological awakening as a result of which Enitharmon is restored to Los and the unity of the disintegrated personality is attained.

Having gone through psychological, moral and ontological awakening (transcendence, integration and participation) Los finally assumes the role of an efficiently functioning ego, which is a "*pontifex oppositorum*; it spans the antitheses, without, however, banishing them" (Szondi–Moser–Webb 39). This central coordinating function of the ego explains why Los was chosen to start the restoration of the pulse of authentic life to the war-torn psyche of Albion and why the Spectre of Urthona, an integral part of Los, is so unlike the other spectres (who are "insane brutish / Deformd" [VII, 84:297–298]) and is called the "Spectre of the Living" (VII, 84:301).

*   *
*

We have now only one Zoa left to study, Urthona's colossal counterpart, the one that appears to be the most compelling and whom Blake had the most to write about: Urizen, Prince of Light.

CHAPTER V

URIZEN AND AHANIA

Fény lakója, isteneknek társa, most
íme, számkivetve élek, eltiltva tőlük.
Turfani töredék, M7

The only feature common to all mental disorder is
the loss of sensus communis and the compensatory
development of a sensus privatus of reasoning.
Immanuel Kant

the grandest Poetry is Immoral the Grandest
characters Wicked
Poetry is to excuse Vice & shew its reason &
necessary purgation
William Blake

Urizen's name has been customarily regarded as a pun on Your-Reason, a word echoing 'horizon', as well as a derivation of the Greek to 'bound' or 'limit' (Bidney 102; Raine *Blake* 2:56), all these implying his main function as the ratio of the five senses, oppressor and restricter.

The name of Urizen's emanation, Ahania, has been most commonly identified as alluding to the Greek wisdom goddess, Athena (e.g., Frye *Fearful* 277; Commentary by Bloom in Blake 908), an etymology strongly supported by Ahania's relationship with Urizen. Another possible reading of the name has been put forth by David Erdman, who postulates that Ahania is the combination of the interjection "Aha!" and "Annia", the name of an Ossianic heroine. Contrary to the usual critical interpretations Daniel Stempel convincingly argues that Ahania is neither Sophia or Wisdom, nor is she Intellectual Pleasure or Desire; her name comes from the Hebrew word for love: *ahavah* (Old Testament) and *agape* (New Testament). Ahavah/agape and charity/caritas express Ahania's true self. "Her love for Urizen, which never falters, . . . is a love that promises fruition, a love that creates 'eternal births' rather than the repetitive cycles of Generation. As Agape, Ahania represents divine love, that form of love which . . . is opposed to Eros; it descends from heaven, unlike the Platonic Eros, which rises toward the divine" (101–102, 112–113).[141]

Urizen is first mentioned by the name on Plate 5 of the *Visions of the Daughters of Albion* but traces of his main characteristics are present as early as the *Poetical Sketches*.[142] As long as Blake's hypothesis was essentially twofold, it allowed for a fairly static character sketch of Urizen, predominantly to be associated with Jehovah and his laws, which from the very beginning were depicted as repressive.

---

[141] Besides convincingly tracing back the etymologies of Ahania, Eleth, Uwe and Ona, Stempel points out that Blake meticulously elaborated his dream-vision. "If my exploration of Blake's etymologies has any value beyond that of unriddling the meaning of names, it is to demonstrate that Blake's myth was far from being a spontaneous effusion of an uncontrolled imagination" (118).

[142] "To Winter". *Tiriel*, too, contains an early version of Urizen. "What strikes us is not that he resembles Lear, but that *Lear resembles him*. He seems to be the mythological ancestor upon whom Shakespeare patterns his historical king" (Youngquist 87).

17. All night beneath the ruins, then their sullen flames faded emerge round the gloomy king.

18. With thunder and fire: leading his starry hosts thro' the waste wilderness he promulgates his ten commands, glancing his beamy eyelids over the deep in dark dismay (*MHH* Plate 26–27)

In the political trilogy, especially in *The Song of Los*, Urizen is beginning to show some traces of the personality he is to become in *The Four Zoas*, although he is still predominantly a political force, incorporating in his character numerous allusions to the fermenting political scene of the last decade of the eighteenth century (while retaining the traits of the Old Testament God).

His stored snows he poured forth, and his icy magazines
He open'd on the deep, and on the Atlantic sea white shiv'ring.
Leprous his limbs, all over white, and hoary was his visage.
Weeping in dismal howlings before the stern Americans
Hiding the Demon red with clouds & cold mists from the earth;
Till Angels & weak men twelve years should govern o'er the strong:
And then their end should come, when France reciev'd the Demons light.
(*SoL* Plate 4)

As the visionary world of the poems becomes more and more refined and the outlines of a threefold system are beginning to emerge, the character of Urizen gets further enrichment. In the psychological trilogy Blake's mythopoeia is outlined and Urizen is depicted as a religious, political, psychological as well as mythological force operating simultaneously – within a single individual and in the universe.

In *The Book of Urizen,* which discloses most of Urizen's character, Blake adumbrates a number of ideas which will later be elaborated in *The Four Zoas*. We learn that Urizen once belonged to the Eternals but has set himself apart from the others; hidden, self-enclosed "I have sought for a joy without pain, / For a solid without fluctuation / Why will you die O Eternals?" (Plate 4). Urizen's fear of futurity and of change, his preference for Being as opposed to Becoming remains one of his most characteristic features. It is a fierce irony that this self-contemplating, abstracted, unprolific shadow of horror, with his laws and creation of the physical universe, is unmistakenly associated with Jehovah:

Lo! I unfold my darkness: and on
This rock, place with strong hand the Book
Of eternal brass, written in my solitude.
Laws of peace, of love, of unity:
Of pity, compassion, forgiveness.
Let each chuse one habitation:
His ancient infinite mansion:
One command, one joy, one desire,
One curse, one weight, one measure
One King, one God, one Law. (*BU* Plate 4)

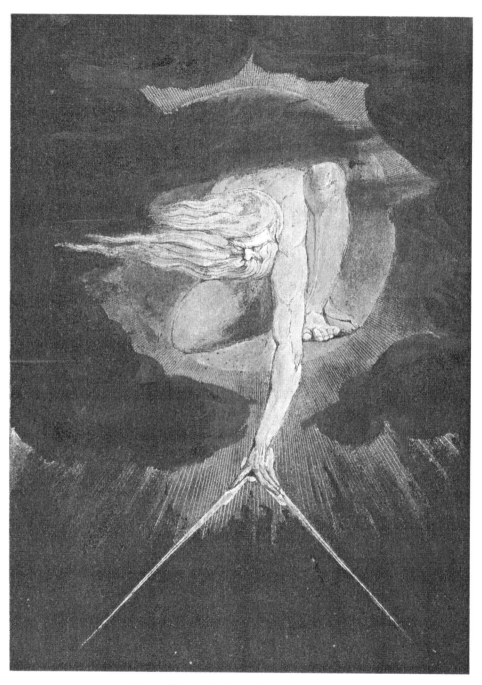

Picture 5 The Ancient Days, Europe (frontispiece)

It is here that Urizen – as clearly as never before – espouses all three implications of his name, as reason, horizon and fixer of boundaries.

Urizen's essential interconnectedness with Los – the interdependence between Intellect and Imagination – is depicted very subtly; Urizen's separation from the Eternals inevitably brings about Los's fall, as the former was rent from his side. It is also Los who forges Urizen a physical body; thus the creation launched by Urizen is completed by him.

It is a striking fact that in *The Book of Urizen*, the Eternals – unlike in *The Four Zoas* – react to Urizen's self-righteousness with intense indignation and it is indeed these Eternals who force Urizen (in Chapter III) to create his vast world against the quenchless flames of their fury. "By destroying the dynamic balance of contraries prevailing in Eternity, Urizen, very much against his intention, has brought about monotonous flux, unpredictable mutability and tormenting instability. These are the objective manifestations of Urizen's progressive spiritual dissociation from Eternal reality" (Kittel 129). Unable to tolerate the sight of the writhing Urizen and Los and horrified at the appearance of the first separate female form, the Eternals complete the Fall by closing down the tent they have erected and by beating down the stakes they make the descent of Intellect and Imagination irreversible.

What comes after the Fall is Urizen exploring his dens (patterned on Satan's journey through Chaos in *Paradise Lost*) and the birth of the all-enwrapping Net of Religion from the sorrows of Urizen's soul. "And the Web is a female in embrio / None could break the Web, no wings of fire" (Plate 25). Urizen is no longer portrayed in the Urizen-Orc dichotomy (hence the admonition that the wings of fire are unable to tear apart Urizen's system) and the bipolar vision gradually gives way to a more diversified myth.

While in the earlier poems the most frequently used words in connection with Urizen were despair, woe, wailing and weeping (later to be explicated) this is now complemented with two new notions. Urizen's alienation from the Eternals finds an eloquent expression in a cluster of symbols of enclosure; the objective correlative for his desire for hiddenness and secresy is the proliferation of caves, caverns and recesses. Organically connected to this is the other group of symbols: nets, webs, traps, binding and enchainment. "Vision has its objective correlative in the landscape, it is born out of caves enclosing chains" (Rotenberg 92).[143] It is interesting to note that both these sets of symbols contribute to the comprehensiveness (and ambivalence) of Urizen, as the first group of images traditionally evokes an allusion to the unconscious – which one would expect to be incongruous with Your-Reason, the rational faculty; much the same as the net and the web, these almost substanceless things appear to be disagreeing with the general idea of Urizen as a character embodying the obsession with materialism.

The Book of Ahania, generally regarded as a continuation of *The Book of Urizen,* is substantially different from the previous myth. With Ahania, Urizen's consort, introduced into the poem, Urizen is no longer depicted as an abstract and fairly generalized figure but – with a new overlay – he is shown as an individual in his family circle. As "in overlays, the earlier version is retained as part of the final entity even when it is rejected" (Wilkie 8),

---

[143] Discussing the symbol of the web and the net, Michael J. Cooke notes that the "web and the net are not entities, but entity-catchers and entity-trappers. Deceptively, yet revealingly, they are made up of a minimum matter and an abundance of nothingness. Their design, in both senses, makes them work, and not their substance" (445).

Urizen's character gets further enrichment. He is reflected through his son, Fuzon, who embodies all the repressed energies of his father, and his counterpart, Ahania, who recalls the days of their unfallen existence and laments for her much-changed companion. The double exposure technique is employed here to accentuate the difference between Eternal Intellect and fallen reason, and to show how "Urizen! Love! / Flower of morning!" (*BA* Plate 4) has become the flower of mourning.

Urizen's relationship with his son is a remarkable example of an unresolved Oedipal conflict: Fuzon's rebellion against his father takes on an unmistakably sexual colouring as he throws his Globe of wrath at Urizen's cold loins and the division of the loins leads to – and is metaphorical of – the separation of Ahania from Urizen. Urizen retorts and smites his son with a poisonous bow subjecting him to Promethean sufferings and crucifying him on the Tree of Mystery, calling up the destiny of Jesus Christ. Much of the Fuzon–Urizen conflict is transported to *The Four Zoas* where Fuzon's fate is echoed in the Los–Orc strife (basically in the allusions to Prometheus) as well as in the Urizen–Orc contention (in the allusions to the crucifixion of Jesus).[144]

The last piece of the psychological trilogy, *The Book of Los*, intersects *The Book of Urizen* at Chapter IV and re-tells the binding of Urizen, this time from Los's point of view, disclosing hardly anything novel about Urizen's character.

Having touched upon the *Book of Urizen*, *The Book of Ahania* and *The Book of Los* we can conclude that – especially in the first two pieces of the trilogy

> we get not only a further enrichment of [Urizen's] personal history but also an immense enrichment of his mythic significance as an agent ubiquitous in human experience. Only at this point can we begin to understand that the tragically fallen form of intellect that Urizen embodies is operating simultaneously, as a single dynamic, in the spheres of politics, religion and the psyche. But his full realization both as character and as a mythic force is not accomplished until Blake works him into the gigantic fabric of *The Four Zoas*. (Wilkie 17–18)

In *The Four Zoas* the first brief mention of Urizen is made by Enitharmon. In her Song of Vala Enitharmon gives her account of the fall, which – in her interpretation – started with Luvah's attempt at seizing Urizen's Horses of Light, metaphorical of the desire of Emotions to usurp the role of Intellect, depicting Urizen – contrary to his portrayal in *The Book of Urizen* – a victim of aggression. As this is the first account of the disintegration of Man (and one does not yet expect more to come), it is likely to be etched in the reader's memory more than the subsequent ones, however significantly it is altered by the sequels. The figure of Urizen is next evoked by Los, who reinforces the notion that in the Eternal world Urizen is associated with thinking/reason and light: "this bright world of all our joy is in the Human Brain. / Where Urizen & all his Hosts hang their immortal lamps" (I, 11:309-310). Contrary to Harold Bloom's assertion that "the reference to Urizen as a prince of light is both an ironic glance at the Enlightenment, and an allusion to Urizen's new role as the Satan of orthodox tradition"(Commentary in Blake 950) we believe that it

---

[144] "A partial realisation of the Orc principle is Fuzon, an inferior poet, so to speak, who leaves Urizen's Egypt but lacks the genius to forge a new orb (in *The Book of Ahania*). He confuses or fuses mere novelty, and consolidates rather than transcends the Urizenic limits" (Quasha 20).

is revealing that Blake – who was undoubtedly familiar with the gnostic idea of light and darkness[145] – assigned this significant attribute to Urizen and would rather consider it as a proof of the integration of Enlightenment values into his visionary universe.

While the first two mention of Urizen were basically recollections concerning his existence in Eternity, he then appears in the midst of the present. In the contentions of Enitharmon and Los, the former turns to Urizen for help:

> Descend O Urizen descend with horse & chariots
>
> . . . .
>
> Eternity groand & was troubled at the Image of Eternal Death
> The Wandering Man bow'd his faint head and Urizen descended
> And the one must have murderd the other if he had not descended (I, 11–12:308–317)

If it had not been for Urizen, the Los–Enitharmon conflict could easily have proved lethal.

It is noteworthy that – quite contary to our expectations based on our previously acquired knowledge of his character – Urizen is introduced into the world of the poem as an agent to bridge division.

However, we do not have to wait long before he starts taking up the characteristics he appeared to slough off for a moment. He declares himself "God from Eternity to Eternity" (I, 12:319) and offers the indignant Los mastery over Luvah and over his starry hosts if only Los "wilt obey" his "awful law"(12:328). Los refuses the pact and in a startling speech he establishes himself – in the vein of *The Book of Urizen* and *The Book of Los* – as a character not unlike Urizen:

> Los answerd furious art thou one of those who when most complacent
> Mean mischief most. If you are such Lo! I am also such
> One must be master. try thy Arts I also will try mine
> For I percieve Thou hast Abundance which I claim as mine (12:329–332)

Urizen takes Los's words as a declaration of war and – revealing himself as "God the terrible destroyer & not the Saviour" (12:337) – launches a dreadful battle, filling the heavens with blood. These disconcerting images are counterbalanced by the Nuptial Song of Los and Enitharmon, at whose wedding we see – the recently militant – Urizen afflicted and thoughtful. With a sudden shift in the narrative we get a new account of the circumstances of the fall, this time from the messengers from Beulah, who relate the events entirely differently from Enitharmon. They claim that the warfare between the Zoas started because of Urizen's foul ambition to usurp Urthona's place, gain dominion over Jerusalem and set himself up as God over all; and they assert that – contrary to Enitharmon's interpretation of the event – it was Urizen who offered his own realm to Luvah in return for his assistance in this plan. (This version is reinforced by Tharmas in the fourth and the Demons in the fifth night.) Like Los before, Luvah declines the alliance (suspecting malice) and attempts to slay Albion as well as Urizen:

---

[145] For Blake and gnosticism see White, Morton and Raine.

> Luvah replied Dictate to thy Equals. am not I
> The Prince of all the hosts of Men nor Equal know in Heaven
> . . . .
> I will remain as well as thou & here with hands of blood
> Smite this dark sleeper in his tent then try my strength with thee (22:504–513)

The first night ends with the wars of Urizen and Luvah which reverse the Eternal Wheels of Intellect, once emblematic of the creative strife of unsundered existence.

The second night discusses the fall of Luvah and his consummation in Urizen's Furnaces of Affliction. This night is the night of victory for Urizen, as the sickening Albion resigns his power to him: "Take thou possession! take this Scepter! go forth in my might" (23:5).

We can notice a gradual refinement in Urizen's portrayal. He is at one moment a self-confident, powerful oppressor who at the other moment suddenly turns into a vulnerable and insecure creature. This ambivalent oscillation between cruel tyrant and atoning, repentant individual (discernible all through this night and indeed all through the poem) is what we shall term as Urizen-cycle. The first exultation over his recently-acquired power is soon replaced by dismay at the sight of chaos and death:

> First he beheld the body of Man pale, cold, the horrors of death
> Beneath his feet shot thro' him as he stood in the Human Brain
> And all its golden porches grew pale with his sickening light
> No more Exulting for he saw Eternal Death beneath
> Pale he beheld futurity (23:11–15)

To ward off total annihilation he starts the creation of the Mundane Shell, using the energies of the consumed Luvah. Urizen as the divine Architect is a peculiar character as from behind his pronounced zeal over his arduous task intermittently lurk out other compelling feelings: woe and despair: "To him his Labour was but Sorrow & his Kingdom was Repentance" (30:208). What comforts him in his moments of despair is the fact that where chaos was now the wondrous outlines of the universe are beginning to emerge.[146]

More importantly, he finds solace in his emanation, Ahania, who appears in the poem as a goddess (sitting in a shrine) to whom Urizen burns incence, a fact that urges Alicia

---

[146] It has been suggested that the very nature of the Mundane shell indicates Urizen's source of comfort. In *The Book of Urizen* – where the notion first appears – Blake explicitly describes it as a womb: "And a roof, vast petrific around, / On all sides He fram'd: like a womb"– so also in *The Four Zoas,* implying that "Urizen is regressing on a cosmic scale, acting out womb-fantasies" (Bidney 122).

Urizen's desire to create a womblike shelter to protect him from the void of futurity is not "at its deepest level a desire to perpetuate the *real* present, but rather a desire to create a static present fashioned in the image of an idealized past" (Bidney 127). This idea is strongly supported by the fact that in Urizen's great speech of repentance of the last night he originally dismissed his preoccupation with the past and remembrance:

> Then Go O dark remembrance I will cast thee forth from these
> Heavens of my brain nor will I look upon remembrance more
> I cast remembrance away & turn my back upon that void
> Which I have made for lo remembrance is in this moment

In the final version, however, Blake revised his original notion and by replacing "remembrance" with "futurity" he shifted the blame from the obsession with the past to the anxiety of the future. (In similar vein see Glausser 196–204.)

Ostriker to conclude that Urizen's attitude very much resembles neo-Platonically inspired sexual reverence which prefers women chaste, exulted and static rather than adjacent and active (159). The Ahania of the following night – though no doubt submissive[147] – is far from being inactive. Responding to Urizen's voicing of his fears of Orc, the Prophetic Boy "Whom Urizen doth serve, with Light replenishing his darkness" (III, 38:15), she urges Urizen to resume his eternal fields of light – which, in other words means that she implores that he give up his present predominance over his fellow Zoas – and presents her account of the fall. Urizen, unable to tolerate the menacing vision, and indeed perhaps the individual voice of his emanation, indignantly casts her out, making their separation – which was for a second foreshadowed in the previous night – complete, and (until Urizen learns better) irrevocable.

> Saying Art thou also become like Vala. thus I cast thee out
> Shall the feminine indolent bliss. the indulgent self of weariness
> The passive idle sleep the enormous night & darkness of Death
> Set herself up to give her laws to the active masculine virtue
> Thou little diminutive portion that darst be a counterpart
> Thy passivity thy laws of obedience & insincerity
> Are my abhorrance. Wherefore hast thou taken that fair form
> Whence is this power given to thee! once thou wast in my breast
> A sluggish current of dim waters. on whose verdant margin
> A cavern shaggd with horrid shades. dark cool & deadly. where
> I laid my head in the hot noon after the broken clods
> Had wearied me. there I laid my plow & there my horses fed
> And thou hast risen with thy moist locks into a watry image
> Reflecting all my indolence my weakness & my death
> To weigh me down beneath the grave into non Entity
> . . . .
> And art thou also become like Vala thus I cast thee out. (43:113–130)

The casting out of Ahania has disastrous consequences, three of which most immediately follow the separation. As Ahania is thrown out, she cracks the universe so laboriously built up by Urizen. As the Mundane shell is crushed into pieces, the mathematically constructed order gives way to chaotic waters; into the ruins of Urizen's world there ride in Tharmas's ceaseless billows. It is noteworthy that the only images that proliferate here are in connection with chaos and fragmentation; it is only here that the the sea image occurs in one primary concentration (Ide, *Image*), implying the onslought of chaos that

---

[147] "And bright Ahania bow'd herself before his splendid feet / O Urizen look on Me. like a mournful stream / I Embrace round thy knees & wet My bright hair with my tears" (III, 37:2–4).

Until the end of the poem Ahania remains entirely submitted to Urizen. She is the only emanation who never enters into an argument and has no sexual conflict with his Zoa. Alicia Ostriker likens her to "those other victims of exacerberated and anxious male intellect, Hamlet's Ophelia and Faust's Grethchen." It is interesting to draw a parallel between Ophelia's "O what a noble mind is overthrown" speech and Ahania's recollection of "those sweet fields of bliss", even as it is worthy of note that Hamlet rejecting Ophelia and slaining her father show remarkable similarities with Urizen casting out Ahania and defying Albion (Ostriker 159, 165).

accompanies the destruction of the physical universe (as well as the close connection of reason and the senses).

The separation of Ahania from Urizen has a serious impact on Enitharmon, too, the only emanation not yet (completely) fallen. With the mildest emanation (Ahania) now disintegrated, the psyche's self-regulating powers seriously weaken and the domineering Female Will (a deteriorated form of Enitharmon) is beginning to appear.

Finally, the casting out of Ahania, thus losing his main source of comfort and inspiration, certainly effects Urizen, who, for the next two nights, seems almost pertified; he sleeps in stoned stupor in the dire ruins of his universe: "A dreamful horrible State in tossings on his icy bed / Freezing to solid all beneath, his grey oblivious form / Strechd over the immense heaves in strong shudders" (IV, 52:171–173). Urizen himself is a ruin, and even as in *The Book of Urizen,* Los is assigned to forge him a body, a task whose consequences have been discussed in the previous chapter.

Although Los's binding of Urizen is transcribed from *The Book of Urizen* with only minor verbal changes to suit the versification of *The Four Zoas,* we witness crucial alterations in context. While in the minor prophecy Urizen's actions – his self-assertion and building of the universe – are utterly negative and he is unequivocally motivated by his own vanity, here it is made explicit that he is a victim of the jealous conspiracy of Los and Enitharmon:

> And Los & Enitharmon were drawn down by their desires
> Descending sweet upon the wind among soft harps & voices
> To plant divisions in the Soul of Urizen & Ahania
> To conduct the Voice of Enion to Ahanias midnight pillow
> Urizen saw & envied & his imagination was filled
> Repining he contemplated the past in his bright sphere
> Terrified with his heart & spirit at the visions of futurity
> That his dread fancy formd before him in the unformd void (II, 34:287–294)

The conceptual changes between the two poems are remarkable. Together with the reassessment of the role of Urizen/reason and Los/imagination – Urizen is no longer depicted as a prevailingly negative character, even as Los is not an exclusively positive figure any more – we find that the cause and consequence of creation have also been shifted. While in *The Book of Urizen* the destructive aspect of creation is emphasized, in *The Four Zoas* it has its positive side, as shall be pointed out shortly. In the first poem Los is compelled by the Eternals to take part in the Creation, in the latter he works at the command of Tharmas and seems to extract sadistic pleasure in his task: "absorbd in dire revenge he drank with joy the cries / Of Enitharmon & the groans of Urizen fuel for his wrath / And for his pity secret feeding on thoughts of cruelty" (IV, 53:191–193). The subtle changes, such as the substantially modified portrayal of Los and Urizen, together with the prime role of Tharmas/senses in an essentially positive creation – at the intersection of the two poems confirm that the assumption of Enlightenment ideas infiltrating into Blake's poems seems to be a tenable premise.

We have seen how Urizen's continued rejection of Ahania turned destructive. As she – like to the emanations in general – is regarded to represent the repressed contents in the Zoa, the process is similar to what Carl Gustav Jung – in *The Structure and Dynamics of the Psyche* – described in the following way: "When the unconscious counteraction is suppressed, it loses its regulating influence. It then begins to have an accelerating and intensifying effect on the conscious process. . . . To begin with, this naturally facilitates the execution of the conscious intentions, but because they are not checked, they may easily assert themselves at the cost of the whole" (quoted in Cramer 528).

It is a remarkable fact that after his separation from Ahania and acquisition of a physical body, Urizen appears – a new phase in the Urizen-cycle – in the fifth night as a character not lacking our sympathy. As he recalls the days of Eternity and repents his past deeds in a most beautiful lament one would anticipate that he is ready for regeneration. At this point image level drops dramatically, pointing to the heightened significance of the passage.

> My fountains once the haunt of Swans now breed the scaly tortoise
> The houses of my harpers are become a haunt of crows
> The gardens of wisdom are become a field of horrid graves
> And on the bones I drop my tears & water them in vain
>
> . . . .
>
> O I refusd the Lord of Day the horses of his prince
> O did I close my treasuries with roofs of solid stone
> And darken all my Palace walls with envyings & hate (63:194–197, 64:211–213)[148]

What follows, however, does not justify our expectation. As Urizen explores his dens in search for Orc in Night the Sixth, he encounters with his daughters and ruthlessly curses them (much as Tiriel and Lear cursed their daughters) "That they may curse & worship the obscure Demon of destruction / That they may worship terrors & obey the violent" (68:44–45).[149] But as he travels through the ruinous world,[150] once so beautiful, his rage and aggression wanes and he soon repents his curse, yet again uncannily transforming into a character capable of rousing our compassion. There is a Sisyphean

---

[148] Harold Bloom interprets "this piercing and self-deceiving ululation" as ironic and claims that Urizen's sorrow over the lost glory is simply a "dangerous nostalgia" (Commentary by Bloom in Blake 957). Our understanding of the part is quite different, as shall be explained later.

[149] Aaron Fogel gives an unparalleled reading of Urizen's cursing of his daughters on Plate 68 (lines 16–25). His approach is so unique that it seems worth taking sufficient place to quote him verbatim:
"This is only one part of a much longer scene in which orc-words – words belonging to a morphemic family based on the principle of /c + vowel + r/ in any order – predominate – and give vocal body to the dialogue between water (liquid sounds like *or*) and rocks (stops like hard *c*). Urizen, here engaged in a search to find Orc whom he feels as a hellish pulsation in himself, confronts these daughters on his journey, and they thwart his interrogation of them. The dialogue of coercion-to-speak is represented, classically enough – as the beating of water against rock, itself obviously Promethean. But what is different and special about Blake's version of this conflict is not the mythology, or the imagery, but the grotesque use of the morphemic patterning to suggest Urizen's moral insanity. As he works himself up to a pitch of hysteria against his daughters the /c + vowel + r/ sounds become more frequent and more clear, until we have *crowns, corruptibility, croakings, care, cords* then the climactic word towards which this list is all rising, *curse*, and then the falling back to *obscure destruction*. Later, when Urizen actually meets Orc, there is much talk about the Crust of Bread and the Obscure as the essence of their relation: false charity and bad art as the outgrowth of the Orc/Urizen mutuality. But in this moment above, a powerful if lurid drama appears in the morphemic undercurrent: when Urizen's hysterical rage comes on he screams unconsciously in Orc-morphemes, to show that his cursing self derives much of its energies from the repressed Orc, a power of psychic change which he experiences only with horror. Change to Urizen is itself Baroque, an exaggerated tension between atrophy and fluidity. Shakespeare's madmen interrupting themselves, speaking a language full of interferences, emerge here revised in Blake's own poetic language. . . . There is a real power in the use of the morphemes to render a 'dialogical' reality, that voice has components of other voices, and that scolding and vituperative voice in particular contains its enemies in alienated, purely material and so unconscious form; the enemy has already invaded the psyche of the speaker and is present there as an unconscious material 'undersong.'" (241).

[150] "In mapping Urizen's journey Blake takes his terminology from the systems of Newton and Descartes" (Fuller 121).

grandeur in Urizen's constantly aberrant efforts to fight against futurity, depicted in his repeated dragging upwards:

> Oft would he sit in a dark rift & regulate his books
> Or sleep such sleep as spirits eternal wearied in his dark
> Tearful & sorrowful state. then rise look out & ponder
> His dismal voyage eyeing the next shpere tho far remote
> Then darting into the Abyss of night his venturous limbs
> Thro lightnings thunders eathquakes & concussions fires & floods
> Stemming his downward fall labouring up against futurity (72:180–186)

His heart sickens at the sight of the horrible ruin, (at once an external landscape and internal mindscape) in which he feels his own fate reverberating, as in his stumbling over hills and vales of torment and fear and falling into the bottomless vacuity the original trauma of the separation and fall is repeated. Harold Bloom notes that these climactic passages of the sixth night describe "more brilliantly than any I know in literature, the onset of the phenomenological disorder, the first signs of man's sick consciousness" (*Blake's* 240). It is ironical that from this sick consciousness there emerges the Web of Religion ("A living Mantle adjoind to his life & growing from his Soul" [73:246]), a process described in *The Book of Urizen*.

Until the much-disputed Night the Seventh, "Blake's epic has lacked a true hero, quite deliberately, for in fallen worlds where all action is equivocal, no hero can exist. The principal protagonist of most of *The Four Zoas* has been Urizen" (Bloom, *Blake's* 246). After his cumbersome journey, Urizen has now reached the Caves of Orc, and the moment is ripe for the encounter of the two extremes, energy (albeit restricted) and ratio (far from being rational). Wilkie and Johnson – somewhat debatably – find that the ensuing

> dialogue between closed-mindedness and unthinking rebelliousness – between age and youth, fascism and anarchy, superego and libido, visiting bureaucrat and jailed hoodlum – is a display of antagonism for its own sake. Though it settles nothing in the plot, it affords exhilarating emotional relief to readers, who recognize primordial forces in the psyche as they act in familiar personality types (143).

It seems more appropriate to suggest that the dialogue serves to accentuate the notion of conflictual undifferentiation, explained previously. Although it is customary to consider Urizen's approach to Orc to be motivated by fear and uncertainty as to the latter's true identity (e.g., Commentary by Bloom in Blake 959), we would rather entertain the possibility that Urizen's intentions here are honest, and his words "Pity for thee movd me to break my dark & long repose / And to reveal myself before thee in a form of wisdom" (VII, 78:57–58) are genuine, rather than hypocritical. This idea is supported by the fact that it is in the moment of the first great enlightenment, at the end of the fifth night, that he sets out to find Orc, as he feels the deep pulsation (caused by the bound demon's awful limbs) shaking his own caverns – an eloquent proof of their essential interconnectedness.[151]

---

[151] Bloom – conversely – interprets Urizen's motive as an "unholy resolution to a sinister quest" (*Blake's* 235).

It is interesting to note that Urizen, with his white hair and iron pen, tracing the wonders of futurity is much more prophetic than the Prophetic Boy, who condemns Urizen's preoccupation with the future.

With a sudden shift, however, Urizen turns into an impostor, declaring himself God and from his books (the most characteristic attribute of his fallen existence) he reads out his in/famous sermon, as hypocritical as it ever can be:

> Compell the poor to live upon a Crust of bread by soft mild arts
> Smile when they frown frown when they smile & when a man looks pale
> With labour & abstinence say he looks healthy & happy
> And when his children sicken let them die there are enough
> Born even too many & our Earth will be overrun
> Without these arts If you would make the poor live with temper
> With pomp give every crust of bread you give with gracious cunning
> Magnify small gifts reduce the man to want a gift & then give with pomp
> Say he smiles if you hear him sigh If pale say he is ruddy
> Preach temperance say he is overgorgd & drowns his wit
> In strong drink tho you know that bread & water are all
> He can afford   Flatter his wife pity his children till we can
> Reduce all to our will as spaniels are taught with art (80:117–129)[152]

From this moment on, up until the end of the eighth night, this aspect of Urizen remains dominant. Winning over Orc does not satisfy him, he starts a bloody war so that all the Sons of Everlasting shall bow down at his feet. To this end he builds the Temple of secret religion in the centre of his empire into which he drags down the Sun "To light the War by day to hide his secret beams by night / For he divided day & night in different orderd portions / The day for the war the night for secret religion in his temple" (VII, 96:36–38). The dragging down of the Sun is repeated by Los in the final night which then signals the beginning of the Last Judgement, while here it seems to imply a culmination of error, presage to the Apocalypse. Simultaneously with the description of Urizen's triumph over nature, in the seventh and eighth nights the crucifixion of Orc and Jesus is repeatedly depicted. Urizen at this most degraded stage is associated with Rahab and it is this connection that causes his ultimate fall. As "Forgetful of his own Laws pitying he began to Embrace / The Shadowy Female" (VIII, 106:420–421)[153] he degenerates into a horrifying beast and in a passage (central to our subsequent analysis of his character), brilliantly synthesizing the previously oscillating vulnerable and irascible facets of Urizen, he is shown as becoming aware of his subordination to the force he sought to contain:

> Oft doth his Eye emerge from the Abyss into the realms
> Of his Eternal day & memory strives to augment his ruthfulness
> Then weeping he descends in wrath drawing all things in his fury
> Into obedience to his will & now he finds in vain
> That not of his own power he bore the human form erect

---

[152] The unmistakable allusions of the passage to contemporary affairs urges Brenda Webster to conclude that "with his increased focus in revision on social evil, Blake tends to diminish Urizen's inner complexity and make him a stereotypical villain somehow responsible for life's evil" (*Blake's Prophetic* 235).

[153] "His pity for the Shadowy Female is the culminating mental error of Deism, representing its exaltation of the supposed virtues of the natural heart" (Commentary by Bloom in Blake 964).

> Nor of his own will gave his Laws in times of Everlasting
> For now fierce Orc in wrath & fury rises into the heavens
> A King of wrath & fury a dark enraged horror
> And Urizen repentant forgets his wisdom in the abyss
> In forms of priesthood in the dark delusions of repentance
> Repining in his heart & spirit that Orc reignd over all
> And that his wisdom servd but to augment the indefinite lust   (107:454–465)

As Urizen declines, Ahania reappears in the poem, lamenting for his lost counterpart. Unlike in *The Book of Ahania,* here she gives a terrifying vision of the present, an apt prelude to the final night.

In the great night of the Last Judgement, the stirring Albion first summons Urizen, to whom he relegated his power at the beginning of Night the Second, and castigates him for all life's evil. Urizen repents and in a majestic speech of enlightenment he casts forth futurity from his brain (realizing that "futurity is in this moment" [121:183]) and lets go of his former enmity with his fellow Zoas, relinquishing his claim to dominate – and, indeed, domineer – over them. Urizen is now ready for regeneration; he throws off his scaly form to reassume the human. He shakes off his aged mantles into the purging fire and "Then glorious bright Exulting in his joy / He sounding rose into the heavens in naked majesty / In radiant Youth" (121:291–293).[154] Even though he has regained much of his original splendour as a shining Apollo, he is not yet complete; he has yet to reunite with Ahania. The reunion is not long in waiting; Urizen embraces the exulting Ahania but she falls dead at the feet of Urizen, a motive genuinely difficult to account for. Perchance their union is premature because the integration of Ahania and Urizen is conditional upon the cooperation of all the Zoas, which will only come when Urizen starts his creative destruction as a Plowman. "Her union with him may represent the self-deception of the mind . . . in an apocalyptic age; the awakened mind becomes too joyful at being able to take pleasure in itself again, and this too-easy gratification cannot survive the intensities of what must be a complex struggle of self-integration" (commentary by Bloom in Blake 965).

The colossal explosion of creative energy (whose like cannot be found anywhere else in English literature [Frye, *Fearful* 305][155]) starts in the brain, where Urizen commences the plowing up of the ruined universe. As in isolation the tearing up of the ground may seem destructive, it is important to note that it is coupled by its contrary, and having prepared the soil to receive the seed, Urizen begins the sowing of the human souls. After

---

[154] Urizen's shaking off his aged mantles is emblematic of, and simultaneous with, his shaking off the accreted overlays.

"Indeed, exactly to the extent that more and more accreted overlays of evil encrust Urizen's personality, like barnacles, does he become a more and more clumsy, complicated, self-entangling machine. For him to regain his true integrated identity he must *slough off* his encrusted overlays, as we see him do in the last two Nights of the *Zoas.* He is able to achieve this redemption of himself because he espouses a kind of pluralism, by virtue of which he does only what is proper to him instead of usurping the roles of the other Zoas and Emanations – in other words, by allowing himself to be one overlay in the total human being instead of incorporating all the overlays into himself. The overlays the fallen Urizen has had to live with are a synthesis but also . . . a merely 'synthetic' synthesis" (Wilkie 19).

[155] Bloom offers a similarly superlative comment when he claims that the final night is "Blake's most exuberant and inventive poetry, probably the most energetic and awesome in the language" (*Blake's* 266).

this is done he takes a temporary rest when Ahania is restored to him, renewing his energies to reap the crop of the human harvest. With the apocalyptic images of Tharmas threshing the crop and Luvah gathering the vintage everything is prepared for Urthona to make the Bread of Ages, the final phase in the Last Judgement. Blake's dream-vision ends with all the four Zoas restored to their proper place and ultimately "all things are changd even as in ancient times" (138:845).

It has previously been suggested that the principal protagonist of the first seven nights was Urizen, who remained an anti-hero up until the beginning of the Apocalypse. The hero finally defined to prepare for the revelation was Los, who, after starting the Last Judgement, disappears from the scene and gives way to the actions of Urizen. No wonder, then, that the very last glimpse we get of the regenerated world of the Zoas presents these two champions of the poem.

> The Sun arises from his dewy bed & the fresh airs
> Play in his smiling beams giving the seeds of life to grow
> And the fresh Earth beams forth ten thousand thousand springs of life
> Urthona is arisen in his strength no longer now
> Divided from Enitharmon no longer the Spectre Los
> Where is the Spectre of Prophecy where the delusive Phantom
> Departed & Urthona rises from the ruinous walls
> In all his ancient strength to form the golden armour of science
> For intellectual War The war of the swords departed now
> The dark Religions are departed & sweet Science reigns (139:846–855)

It is worthy of note that the glory of Urthona is straightforwardly depicted, even as his role in procuring the restoration of Albion is repeatedly accentuated, while Urizen is implicitly referred to in the last line, just as the indispensable part he plays in the regeneration is subtly concealed behind the actions of a genuinely ambiguous character, as shall be demonstrated presently.

We shall, as before, use the figures of the Szondi test as parallels in our understanding certain features of Urizen's character. He shows striking parallels with the *Category of Purism, Moralism and Atonement* of the paroxysmal/convulsive drive – also termed as the startle drive (Lukács, *Szondi* 28). This category is the most important and unitary one of all categories with regard to the personality quality of its members (Szondi, *Experimental* 184). As this is the category, whose main features – to a varying extent – are discoverable in each and every individual (Szondi, *Káin* 51), it is no longer surprising that Urizen (and not Los) gets so central a role in the Apocalypse of the final night; the poem's ultimate concern is with the "resurrection to unity, with the restoration of full humanity to *every kind and sort of human being. The Four Zoas* is, in the end, not a justification of Blake's or the artist's ways but the justification of God's ways – which are the actions in time and eternity of the Eternal Man in all of us" (Wilkie and Johnson 237, emphasis added), a supreme example of Blake's self-transcendence as a Romantic artist, and a beautiful rendering of the Romantic aesthetic of art for man's (and for life's) sake – which also explains Los's relative insignificance.

We have seen that the most characteristic features of the fallen Urizen were his violent explosions and the subsequent repentance, similarly to the people of this category, otherwise called *homines paroxysmales* (Szondi, *Káin* 51). The interpretation of this category is centered in the "paroxysmal storing up and sudden release of energy. In the Szondi test, epilepsy is interpreted psychologically as the purest manifestation of the aggressive outburst" (Deri 88–89).[156] Epilepsy has of old been called *morbus sacer* (implying the compelling religious needs, which denote the epileptic character), well corresponding to the figure of Urizen. The mounting aggressiveness and increasing irritability – which sometimes reach a point when the person feels a compulsion to injure somebody in his environment – is terminated by the actual attack, sometimes followed by coma, a process clearly delineated in the Urizen-Ahania conflict in the third night, when Urizen's growing wrath (hence Ahania's intermittent remarks in the middle of her speech: "Why roll thy clouds in sick'ning mists"; "frown not Urizen: but listen to my Vision" as well as "O Urizen why art thou pale at the visions of Ahania" [41:71, 41:84, 42:91]) reaches its climax and he cruelly casts out his emanation:

> She ended. for [from] his wrathful throne burst forth the black hail storm
> . . . .
> Then thunders rolld around & lightnings darted to & fro
> His visage changd to darkness & his strong right hand came forth
> To cast Ahania to the Earth he siezd her by the hair
> And threw her from the steps of ice that froze around his throne (42–43:108–112)

The coma-phase following the attack coincides with the stonified sleep and total inertia of Urizen in the succeeding night. The last stage of the process, organically bound to the previous ones, is characterized by the individual's strict emotional control of his aggressive tendencies. This hyper-ethical – often hyper-religious – stage is the phase of atonement (Szondi, *Káin* 97, Deri 88–89). This atonement of Urizen (which immediately follows the wrath-outburst-coma-sequence) is described in his great lament at the end of Night the Fifth:

> O Fool to think that I could hide from his all piercing eyes
> The gold & silver & costly stones his holy workmanship
> O Fool could I forget the light that filled my bright spheres
> Was a reflection of his face who calld me from the deep
> I well remember for I heard the mild & holy voice
> Saying O light spring up & shine & I sprang up from the deep
> He gave to me a silver scepter & crownd me with a golden crown
> & said Go forth & guide my Son who wanders on the ocean
> I went not forth. (64:214–222)[157]

The same process is depicted in the next night, when Urizen curses his daughters and then repents his rash curse, with the exception that here the phase of atonement is even

---

[156] Bidney notes that Urizen is "possessed by a daimonic rage for order, a rage with an irrational origin . . . and with predictably irrational consequences" (102).

[157] As it has previously been mentioned, we cannot agree with Bloom's interpretation of the passage as a hypocritical lament, but rather presume that Urizen's words are genuine and his transformation is comprehensible and consistent as it is congruous with his (paroxysmal-epileptiform) character.

more distinctly pious, as from Urizen's laments the Web of Religion is born. It is this last phase that is most important in the *Category of Purism, Moralism and Atonement*. The category "reflects those aspects of the personality which are closely bound to the development of the superego" (Deri 89), which Blake scholars unequivocally associate with Urizen. Members of the category are concerned with questions about "good" and "bad" in general; "the highly socialized ones turn into moralists, purists who are obsessed by the urge to purge and cleanse. They purge language, art, literature, styles, morals and 'improve' people and society" (Szondi, *Experimental* 185), hence much of the antagonism between Urizen and Luvah, and Urizen and Orc as well as the notion of Urizen as the lawgiver. This constantly recurring circle of wrath-outburst-coma-atonement is what we have termed as a specific Urizen-cycle in the poem.

Characteristic tendencies of this group of people, such as the ambition to be something great and to accomplish something of lasting importance are all discernible in Urizen's repeated claim that he is God and in his building of the Temple of secret religion. The most distinctive feature, however, which makes Urizen an apt example of the category is that "there is a certain stickiness to these personalities, which renders them incapable of ever leaving an object they once attach themselves.... This clinging to objects is a highly characteristic trait of members in [this] category" (Szondi, *Experimental* 186). The objects Urizen clings to in his fallen existence are his books.[158] Ever since the first mention of them in the sixth night, they remain inseparable from the Zoa. He carries them along as he drags through the ruined universe, no matter what difficulties they may present on this agonizing journey:

> But still his books he bore in his strong hands & his iron pen
> For when he died they lay beside his grave & when he rose
> He siezd them with a gloomy smile for wrapd in his death clothes
> He hid them when he slept in death when he revivd the clothes
> Were rotted by the winds the books remaind still unconsumd
> Still to be written & interleavd with brass & iron & gold (71:167–172)

In the seventh night the books get a heightened emphasis, as Urizen is depicted as compulsively tracing his books ("Thundering & hail & frozen iron haild from the Element / Rends thy white hair yet thou dost fixd obdurate brooding sit / Writing thy books." [79:79–81]) and reading out his moral teachings. (The image is repeated seven times in the first 170 lines!) It is only in the overall destruction of the Last Judgement that "The books of Urizen unroll with dreadful noise" (118:33) and consume – together with the Spectre of Urthona, Tirzah and Rahab – in the raving fire.

The process whereby the the crude affects (like rage, hatred, resentment, vindictiveness and jealousy) accumulate and explosively discharge and then change into a tendency toward goodness and righteousness was termed by Szondi as the *Cain-Moses dialectics* (our Urizen-cycle), in which the last – atonement – phase is metaphorically called the Moses-complex (*Káin* 97, 269). Szondi claims – and we have indeed seen the same notion confirmed in the character of Urizen – that good and evil, sacred and profane, Cain and Moses are not negations but contraries, which creatively complement each other in the

---

[158] About Urizen and his books see Paul Mann, "*The Book of Urizen* and the Horizon of the Book."

same person.[159] A very similar idea is put forth in esoteric symbology, in which Cain is regarded to be identical with Jehovah or the 'Lord God' (Blavatsky 67). In Szondi's system the convulsive drive (also called the ethics drive) is personified by Moses, who is Cain turned into Abel (*Káin* 94).

It is striking to see that Urizen, too, is modelled on Moses, not only in the poems (hence his giving of the Ten Commandments and preoccupation with his books on morality) but also in the paintings. The visual portrayal of Urizen confirms his association with Moses, as in all the paintings he is almost like a mirror-image of Michaelangelo's Moses. The first appearance of this typical face (in *Satan, Sin and Death* as well as *Moses Receiving the Law*) is around 1780, which is when Blake is out of his apprenticeship to James Basire (1772–1779) and is beginning to develop his unique style and figures. He later uses the same figure chiefly to depict Shakespearean subjects, notably for the illustrations to *King Lear* (*Lear Grasping his Sword* of 1788), upon which he seems to have modelled Tiriel, an early version of Urizen. From the mid-1790s, simultaneously with his more and more frequent appearance in the poems, the character is variously called in the pictures as Urizen, Elohim and Moses.

What is the significance of the fact that Urizen is modelled upon Moses, even as the corresponding Szondian category is personified by the Old Testament prophet.

The most immediate explanation for the Urizen-Moses congruity is Blake's portrayal of his Zoa as the giver of the Ten Commandments, a lawgiwer who thereby imposes intolerable limits on Mankind. Yet, this restrictive function is only part of what he stands for. Much more importantly, with the Ten Commandments the rule of the priests ended, in other words, with Moses a *direct* and *personal relationship* between *God and Man* started – which was what Blake celebrated all through his poetry. The intimate relationship with

---

[159] Urizen's ambiguous actions recall Yahweh's words to Jeremiah: "See, I have this day set thee over the nations and over the kingdoms, to root out, and to pull down, and to destroy, and to throw down, to build, and to plant" (The Book of the Prophet Jeremiah 1:10).

The duality of Urizen's (paroxysmal) character is also noted by Vincent A. De Luca, who claims that the key term in the discourse of 18th-century sublime, "astonishment", encompasses Urizen's whole program, as his actions are as ambiguous as the term itself (which Blake used more frequently – 51 times – than any other major poet between 1660 and 1830). "Astonishment" simultaneously implies an internal and external phenomenon; it denotes a psychological state as well as refers – by virtue of its form – to the powers of vegetated nature: thunder (from which it is derived) and stone (which it resembles in sound) both of which are unmistakenly associated with Urizen. His voice of thunder is carefully repeated to accentuate the Urizen-Jehovah identity. His association with stone is supported by a number of instances. Urizen's stonified sleep following his separation from Ahania, his petrified heart ("be your hearts harder than the nether millstone" [VII, 80:112]) and his enrootedness in his iron rock (in Night the Seventh) are but a few such instances. Extratextually, the Urizen-Moses parallel implies his connection with stone.

De Luca points out that Blake shows a strikingly persistent allegiance to Burke, whose definition of 'astonishment' – as formulated in *A Philosophical Enquiry into the Origin of Our Ideas of the Sublime & the Beautiful* – is as follows:

"The passion caused by the great & sublime in *nature*, when those causes operate most powerfully, is Astonishment; & astonishment is that state of the soul, in which all its motions are suspended, with some degree of horror. In this case the mind is so entirely filled with its object, that it cannot entertain any other, nor by consequence reason on that object which employs it. Hence arises the great power of the sublime, that far from being produced by them, it anticipates our reasonings, & hurries us on by an irresistable force" (quoted in De Luca 101).

"Astonishment", then, incorporates in itself a double potential: it either immobilizes or releases. A thunder can not only petrify but may also crack open the stones "releasing our buried powers to freedom. . . . The 'astonishment' produced by this clarifying thunder encompasses the moment when surfaces and opacities are burst to reveal the infinite potential within" (102). This bipolar concept of astonishment finds eloquent expression in Urizen's harrowing in the Last Judgement.

God, albeit regulated by uniform laws imposed on Man from without seems to encompass the whole program of Urizen[160] and account for his portrayal as a paroxysmal character, within whom the Moses and the Cain traits oscillate. In his character the possibility of regeneration and the pain of generation are united.

The next few pages shall be devoted to the evaluation of Urizen's figure, discussing him in the light of the Cain-Moses dialectics with the intention of redeeming him from the role of a villain which has traditionally been assigned to him.[161] The problem with such interpretations is that they take into consideration only parts of Urizen's actions in the poem – those which correspond to the accumulation and discharge of the crude affects and look at the succeeding atonement phase as mere hypocricy or fierce irony (on Urizen's and Blake's part respectively).[162] These critics regard the fall, brought about by Urizen, as a tragic incident, which shatters the original harmony and inflicts unnecessary pain and suffering on Man. The characters' intermittent nostalgic accounts apparently support this notion. They all describe "those blessed fields / Where memory wishes to repose among the flocks of Tharmas" (II, 34:325–326). The constant collation of the present world with those fields of bliss serve to accentuate the sense of loss and degeneration. Yet, a closer look at the text reveals that the ideal(ized) state of Eternity cannot be identical with the highest ontological state, Eden. Urizen's reminiscences,

> Once how I walked from my palace in gardens of delight
> The sons of wisdom stood around the harpers followd with harps
> Nine virgins clothd in light composd the song to their immortal voices
> And at my banquets of new wine my head was crownd with joy (V, 64:198–201)

closely resemble the scene depicted on Illustration I of the *Illustrations of the Book of Job* (with the exception that in the picture the musical instruments are already silenced, which foreshadows the nearing fall). To consider the Zoas' original place as one of complete harmony is self-delusion – even as it proved to be in the case Job – for three good reasons.

1. Eternity is the internalized state of the *Songs of Innocence* (hence the striking similarities in their imagery), the unconscious world of precarious balance.

2. Spiritual Eden for Blake is fourfold, while we learn from the Spectre that Eternity was threefold ("If we unite in one, another better world will be / Opend within your heart

---

[160] A supreme example for this dual aspect is to be found on Plate 4 of *The Book of Urizen*. Urizen/Moses gave
    Laws of peace, of love, of unity:
    Of pity, compassion, forgiveness.
    Let each chuse one habitation:
    His ancient infinite mansion:
    One command, one joy, one desire,
    One curse, one weight, one measure
    One King, one God, one Law.
In the first two lines we can find everything Blake celebrated, regulated by degenerating laws.

[161] For a typical evaluation of Urizen as tyrant and oppressor see Abrahams 14–30. Charu Sheel Shing also claims that the forces of good spring from Los and Orc, while the evil forces are typified chiefly by the fallen Urizen (138). Harold Bloom, too, tends to identify Urizen with an oppressive sky-god and fearful limiter of desire (*Blake's* passim).

[162] Wilkie and Johnson – somewhat dissenting from common critical concensus – explain that Urizen recognize the threat of chaos but feels obliged to make his dismal visions come true. His "psychology is that of Jonah or any prophet of doom who ought to want to be proved wrong but in fact wants, egocentrically and irrationally, his presence to be vindicated; the result is a dynamic of self-fulfilling prediction" (55–56).

Picture 6 Illustrations for the Book of Job (1826)

& loins & wondrous brain / Threefold as it was in Eternity" [VII, 85:354–356]), which is the world of Beulah, land of delusions, one step below the perfect condition, as has been pointed out previously.

    3. Finally, the most definitive argument, which makes a revaluation of Urizen's role inevitable, is that the regenerated Albion, who is born in the colossal final night, is not the same as the one who had to fall because of the war among his members[163]; an important

---

[163] This idea is supported by the illustrations, too. The design for the frontispiece depicts a male nude "who resembles Blake's soaring figures, but he does not look energetic enough to have broken his bonds; if we imagine ourselves looking at him . . . from above we catch an aerial view of a sleeper lying in his unquiet bed. He is radiating light, the Divine Vision, but his eyes are closed to it" (Wilkie and Johnson 9). At the end of the poem, however, a New Man is born, himself the Divine Vision.

change has taken place: Luvah and Vala have been assigned a new place within the resurrected Man, "You shall forget your former state return o Love in peace / Into your place the place of seed not in the brain or heart" (126:364–365). As the final night is one jubilant exultation over the birth of the Eternal Man, we can rightly conclude that the fall – with all the torments it included – was not meaningless, and instead of the original *coincidencia oppositorum*, in the final night *complexio oppositorum* is achieved, through the instrumentality of Urizen. This idea of ascending to a higher ontological state at the end of a circuitous journey dominated the thinking of many of Blake's German contemporaries, among them Schelling, who formulated the same notion: "I posit God as the first and the last, as Alpha and Omega, but as Alpha he is not what he is as Omega; and insofar as he is the first . . . he cannot, strictly speaking, be called God; unless one were to say expressly 'the undeveloped God,' *Deus implicitus,* since, as Omega, he is *Deus explicitus"* (quoted in Abrams 186). The central function of Urizen as the agent in the divination of Albion is explicitly formulated in the inscription of the manuscript of *The Four Zoas*: "Unorganizd Innocence, An Impossibility / Innocence dwells with Wisdom but never with Ignorence" (Blake 697).

In Blake's painting, *The Whirlwind: Ezekiel's Vision of the Four Zoas,* the Zoas are depicted as four male profiles, two on either side of the picture. As has been previously stated, the definitive trait of Ezekiel's Zoas is their unswerving motion; they respond unfalteringly to the divine will that commands them, "Their wings were joined to one another; they turned not when they went; they went everyone straight forward" (1:9). Goldsmith, analysing the picture, claims that with the double exposure of the Zoas, Blake tried to fabricate the illusion of a fourfold wholeness, but he only made manifest a set of internal contradictions, as "one cannot have straightforward motion without sacrificing the straightforward motion" (158). He implies that – by virtue of the illustration – one of the Zoas has to move backwards. The Zoa he identifies as bound to a retrograde motion is Urizen, whose withdrawal triggered the fall into generation. We shall try to argue that this apparent retrocession may be most progressive, and Urizen, whose face is concealed from us, may be the only one facing the Divine Entelechy, watching over Man unseen in the background.

The idea of the redemptive value of suffering and that the unruly affects serve a larger rational – albeit unforeseen – scheme was most remarkably summerized by Blake's famous contemporary, Hegel, whose system was a point of departure for a number of Blake scholars.[164] Blake's simultaneity of reference to internal and external events in *The Four Zoas* makes such a comparison especially apt. Philip Pomper's account of Hegel is easily applicable to *The Four Zoas* of Blake:

---

[164] Thomas J. Altizer in *The New Apocalypse* takes Hegel as a model for a *theological* explication of Blake, emphasizing the internalized spiritual struggle within the individual to find the divine inside. In his study he focuses primarily on Luvah. David Punter's *Blake, Hegel and Dialectic,* on the other hand, concentrates on the *social* dimension which, he claims, offers the key to the historical situation of dialectic. Lorraine Clark suggests that Blake is both Hegelian and anti-Hegelian: "Briefly, my argument is that in his new focus on the struggle of Los and the Spectre in *The Four Zoas, Milton* and *Jerusalem,* Blake turns from a Hegelian 'both-and' dialectic of Orc and Urizen in his early works to something very like a Kierkegaardian 'either/or'. This new dialectic of Los and the Spectre . . . is in fact a complex inversion of the Orc-Urizen dialectic" (2).

For a more detailed discussion of the Hegelian, anti-Hegelian debate see Clark 35–36.

Occassionally, Hegelian terms, like "Being" and "Becoming", come up in Blake scholarship, but they are used to refer to different concepts. While Northrop Frye proposes that "Being" and "Becoming" approximate Blake's Orc and Los (*Fearful* 247), David Bidney uses them to denote Urizen and Urthona/Los, respectively (passim).

Picture 7 The Whirlwind: Ezekiel's Vision of the Four Zoas (1803–05)

Hegel imagined history as a process and structured its development dialectically in a way that anticipates the psychoanalytic intelligentsia's theories of history. He made the kinds of connections between mental process and historical development that psychohistorians make in their language of psychoanalysis. If there is a psychology informing Hegel's dialectic and phenomenology of spirit, then it is reasonable to speculate that the appeal of his vision of history is in some way associated with it – that what appeals in it, in fact, is an intuitive developmental psychology. (26)

The notion of the necessity of pain and destruction for the betterment of the world existed well before Hegel's *Phenomenology*; it informed the Hellenic world, the teachings of Hermetic philosophy, the apocryphal apocalypses as well as the Talmud.[165] The

---

[165] For a detailed discussion of related matters see Eliade. The inevitability of agony is there in the writings of the Antinomian Abiezer Coppe, whose ideas show remarkable similarities with Blake's: "But behold, behold, he is now risen with a witness, to save *Zion* with vengeance, or to confound and plague all things into himself; who by his mighty Angell is proclaiming (with a loud voyce) That Sin and Transgression is finished and ended; and everlasting righteousnesse brought in; and the everlasting Gospell preaching; Which everlasting Gospell is brought in with most terrible earth-quakes, and heaven-quakes" (quoted in Morton 46).

Kabbalistic axiom, *Demon est Deus Inversus*, warns against a too hasty depreciation of Urizen's character. In the universe of the Zoas, he is cast the role of the evil, hence the predominance of 'woe', 'despair', 'wailing' and 'weeping' whenever he appears – he is weeping because of what he has done, others are weeping because of what he has done to them. It is an uncongenial task Urizen is assigned, though indispensable if Man is to become God. "If God is any thing he is Understanding. . . . Understanding or Thought is not natural to Man it is acquired by means of Suffering & Distress i.e Experience. Will, Desire, Love, Rage, Envy, & all other Affections are Natural. but Understanding is Acquired But Observe. without these is to be less than Man" *(Annotations to Swedenborg's Divine Love and Divine Wisdom).*[166] As Immanuel Kant summed up in his essay on the *Conjectural Origin of the History of Man*, the replacement of instinctual behaviour (the golden age of Tharmas) by rational thought (Urizen's world), seen from the individual's standpoint, resulted in a host of evils, distress and pain, but from the stance of the human race the assertion of the rule of reason is an indispensable step in the progress towards perfection. Urizen's destructive benevolence, then – the first two phases of his paroxysmal character – is in the service of an unquestionably decisive process: the divination of Man. It is now understandable why Luvah/Jesus is almost inseparable from Urizen; this intimate connection accounts for the former's lack of definition. Urizen, too, is inseparable from Luvah. Urizen is the redeemer in a specifically Blakean sense as through his agency Luvah – the historical, vegetated Jesus – is crucified and the only true Christ, the Divine Image, is incarnated.[167]

The pictorial evidence to justify Urizen's "crime" against Luvah is *The Last Judgement* picture of the Rosenwald Collection. While in the first two versions of the same event (*A Vision of the Last Judgement* of the Stirling Maxwell Collection and *The Vision of the Last Judgement* of the Egremont Collection) the cross is exalted into the heavens whereas Satan – enwound by the Serpent – is falling down, in the third drawing a crucial change is discernible. The cross is no longer exalted into heaven but is falling down, implying that the cross – commonly associated with the vegetated body of Christ – does not belong to

---

[166] Carl Gustav Jung – in "The Psychology of the Child Archetype" – comes to a similar conclusion: "It is only separation, detachment, and agonizing confrontation through opposition that produce consciousness and insight" (quoted in Cramer 527).

[167] This notion is justified by the following – inserted and then deleted – lines from Night the First (textual Notes in Blake 825):

> we immortal in our own strength survive by stern debate
> Till we have drawn the Lamb of God into a mortal form
> And that he must be born is certain for One must be All
> And comprehend within himself all things both small & great
> We therefore for whose sake all things aspire to be & live
> Will so recieve the Divine Image that amongst the Reprobate
> He may be devoted to Destruction

Urizen's redemptive role is even more explicitly formulated in *Milton* (Plate 27:55–61):

> But in Eternity the Four Arts: Poetry, Painting, Music,
> And Architecture which is Science: are the Four Faces of Man.
> Not so in Time & Space: there Three are shut out, and only
> Science remains thro Mercy: & by means of Science, the Three
> Become apparent in Time & Space, in the Three Professions
> Poetry in Religion: Music, Law: Painting, in Psychic & Surgery:
> That Man may live upon Earth till the time of his awaking

(and indeed has no place in) the resurrected world. The World of Eden may not commence until Luvah has perished through the agency of Urizen.

The paradoxical notion of Urizen as redeemer is in account with the idea of the Oriental church fathers who – as Elias Canetti noted – "claimed that Christ was uglier than any man who ever lived. For in order to redeem mankind, he had to take upon himself all of Adam's sins and even his physical blemishes" (quoted in Bidney 68).[168]

The Urizen-Christ association is virtually depicted in one picture from approximately 1820. Of the four extant copies of *Jerusalem,* three are black and white and delineate God in a Satanic form, but the latest copy is printed in colour and portray the Creator as the radiating Jesus, the Saviour.[169]

One more interesting coincidence needs to be quoted which substantiates our hypothesis of Urizen as Redeemer. Paul Youngquist – quite unappreciatively – notes that Urizen embodies pure self-consciousness stripped of feeling and reduced to an automatic bodily response, and in his character he prefigures Camus's Meursault (94). It is striking that Camus, in his preface to the 1958 edition of *L'Étranger,* remarks that Meursault is the only Christ we deserve (1929).[170]

It has previously been pointed out that 'stone' is closely connected with Urizen. The significance and role of stone in alchemy (whose teachings can be found all through Blake's poetry) appears to be the same as that of Urizen in *The Four Zoas*: it is allied to Logos and is phallic/creative in nature.[171]

The creation of the Mundane Shell, we learn from Blake, "was an act of Mercy" (*VLJ,* page 91). Blake scholars – following Frye, who seems to have taken over the idea from Jacob Boehme – unanimously explain that the Creation was an act of Mercy because – though part of the Fall – with its stability and permanence it put a limit to the Fall, forming a "barrier between our weak struggling lives and the total annihilation of all being in chaos" (*Fearful* 138). Instead of this argument we would rather propose another interpretation. It may seem just as appropriate to see the creation in the context of myths. Eliade notes that the healing rites point to the contention that life cannot be restored; it

---

[168] Jorge Louis Borges also tells an enigmatic tale of Judas, who is identical with Christ (168–176).

[169] This same notion is subtly implied in the heightened significance of Urizen's *iron pen* in Night the Sixth. The iron pen, Urizen's instrument of putting down his words of wisdom, not only recalls Job's lament (19:23–25): "Oh that my words were now written! oh that they were printed in a book! That they were graven with an iron pen and lead in the rock forever! For I know *that* my redeemer liveth, and *that* he shall stand at the latter *day* upon the earth", but is later – in *The Everlasting Gospel* – given to Jesus' hands to put down the crucial sentence: "Upon his heart with Iron pen / He wrote Ye must be born again". (For a detailed discussion of the "iron pen" – including its discussion as Blake's tool of his trade – see Essick 209–237.)

[170] " ... j'avais essayé de figurer dans mon personnage le seul christ que mon méritons" (Camus 1929).

[171] See Hárs 77.

can only be re-created by the reiteration of the cosmogonical act. The reiteration of this cosmic creation is expected to heal physical as well as spiritual maladies (123).[172]

As Albion is sick, Urizen's act of creation is indeed a redemptive act of Mercy as it essentially effects Albion's recovery, which – in other words – means the Ancient Man's birth into a higher ontological state.

We have seen that what is called sickness (death or sleep) on the level of the individual/ microcosm is – on the level of the macrocosm – human history. Norman O. Brown,[173] a notable contemporary psychohistorian shows a striking allegiance to the Blakean idea of the interconnectedness of history and the diseased individual. He believes that history is a product of the innate weakness of the human ego and assumes that "other animal species are normal precisely because they do not have histories. Only man, the neurotic animal, has a history and he has a history because he represses himself. Repression creates the 'dialectic of neurosis', which in turn is the dialectic of history. Historical cultures are all symptom-formations" (Pomper 130). Brown points out that in order to find a way out of history – that is to recover from the deadly sleep Albion has lapsed into – one has to display the weakness and its symptoms, which is precisely what happens in *The Four Zoas*.

For all their similarities, one crucial difference between the two concepts needs to be noted. While for Brown the remedy is to restore to man his animal nature, which is the homeostatic, unconflicted and ahistorical condition of animals in a state of nature (dualism, Brown asserts, signifies conflict, neurosis and continuous struggle; in short: history [Pomper

---

[172] Urizen's indispensable and ultimately positive role as creator is confirmed by Blake's definition of the "sublime as the art of distinct line and formal clarity" (Essick 150). As we read in Night II:

Mighty was the draught of Voidness to draw Existence in
Terrific Urizen strode above, in fear & pale dismay
He saw the indefinite space beneath & his soul shrunk with horror
His feet upon the verge of Non Existence (24:18–21)
In the place of the indefinite void Urizen builds the Mundane Shell:
But infinitely beautiful the wondrous work arose

. . . .
                    & Urizen comforted saw
The wondrous work flow forth like visible out of the invisible (32:240; 33:259–260)

As opposed to the blurred colours of Tharmas/painting (hence his indefiniteness and constant association with water), Urizen creates firm outlines. "Outlines," Péter Egri notes, "mark, separate and determine visual phenomena." As a rule "visual demarcation develops into intellectual discrimination" (108-109); the firm outlines are the visual representation of Intellect. Urizen as a Divine Architect embodies Blake's leading aesthetic imperative:

"The great and golden rule of art, as well as of life, is this: That the more distinct, sharp, and wiry the bounding line, the more perfect the work of art; and the less keen and sharp, the greater is the evidence of weak imitation, plagiarism, and bungling. . . . The want of this determinate and bounding form evidences the want of idea in the artist's mind . . . . What is it that builds a house and plants a garden, but the definite and determinate? What is it that distinguishes honesty from knavery, but the hard and wiry line of rectitude and certainty in the actions and intentions. Leave out this line and you leave out life itself; all is chaos again, and the line of the almighty must be drawn upon it before man or beast can exist" (*DesC* 63–64).

Outline and Urizen: these aesthetic and ethical concerns are of paramount importance in Blake's writings.

[173] Norman O. Brown identifies himself as dialectician. He uses the dialectical architectonics, which organizes a process of progressive change around conflicts. Dialecticians believe that without contradiction or negation, conflict or opposition, development lacks a dynamic principle. Brown views history as a "forward-looking *récherche du temps perdu*,"and – faithful to Hegel – sees history as the phenomenology of the mind. The dialectical architectonic believes in the mind's ability to restore itself and transposes the inner struggle for self-healing to history (Pomper 132; Botond 80–86). The idea of *endopsychic anthropomorphism* is where Brown's and Blake's ideas most conspicuously overlap.

132]), Blake believes that 'once out of nature' and history, Man will live in a continuous intellectual strife. Blake's ultimate Brotherhood of Eden is *philadelphia,* which involves conscious acts and an unceasing mental effort to love brothers rather than *adelphos,* a static state of brotherly community (Iazumi). What is born in the final night of the poem is this supreme state of higher innocence, in which historical contingency has been eliminated, a state in which history/disease/death has come to an end. "From the earliest apocalyptic texts of Judeo-Christian Scripture to the experiments with apocalyptic representation by romantic writers, and on to various rhetorical strands within postmodernism itself, the idea of the end of history has often been bound up with the promise of an *aesthetic* space relieved of historical determinants" (Goldsmith 1–2). In the Apocalypse of the last night this aesthetic space is achieved when Urthona, the eternal Artist "rises from the ruinous walls / In all his ancient strength to form the golden armour of science / For intellectual War" (139:852–854). Blake's idea of the higher innocence, then, is very close to Schiller's notion of the aesthetic state, as it is in this state alone, claim both, that we experience infinite human potentiality; "here alone do we feel reft out of time, and our human nature expresses itself with purity and integrity, as though it had as yet suffered no impairment through the intervention of external sources" (quoted in Goldsmith 8).[174]

Although the supreme state is closely associated with Urthona, the Artist, it is notable that he alone would be incapable of attaining it. It has recently been pointed out that the most fundamental idea about the aesthetic space is that it is self-contained and is completely devoid of any historical determinants. As Los is the Eternal Prophet, he is closely associated with classical prophecy, in which history is always divinely motivated and implicitly endless. "Prophecy typically defines the furthest extent of redemption as a return to life as normal: 'They shall build houses and inhabit them; they shall plant vineyards and eat their fruit' (Isaiah 65:21)" (Goldsmith 31). Los, the prophet, then, is not able to reach the ultimate aesthetic phase; he – by himself – could only lead Albion back to Beulah where he fell from.

Albion's life has been so corrupted that more radical action is needed. This more radical action is apocalyptic redemption, which differs from prophecy in its markedly different understanding of history. Apocalyptic redemption occurs as the abrupt end to history, when history has been so usurped by evil forces that it cannot function as the medium of divine activity (Goldsmith 31).

The agent of this apocalyptic redemption is Urizen, a premise supported by two good arguments.

Apocalypse "requires an itinerant prophet outside institutional stability and vigilance" (Goldsmith 54), a requirement undoubtedly fulfilled by Urizen, whose endless and painful travels – after his fall from Eternity – is so meticulously described in the poem.

The other point to substantiate the hypothesis that it is Urizen who brings about apocalyptic redemption is the fact that apocalypse is a "bookish" phenomenon; by the time John writes his apocalypse, the idea of an authoritative book has become indispensable to a vision of final retribution and salvation.[175] At the end of The Book of Daniel, the prophet is ordered to "shut up the words, and seal the book, *even* to the time of the end"

---

[174] For a detailed discussion of Schiller, Frye, Bloom and Derrida in connection with apocalypse and the idea of an ahistoric aesthetic see Goldsmith 8–19. On related matters Abrams 56–65.

[175] In a compelling chapter – History Ends in a Book: Biblical Apocalypse and the Suppression of Difference – Steven Goldsmith meticulously points out the essential interconnectedness of 'apocalypse' and 'book' (27–84).

(12:4). The opening of the book and the end of history are considered as simultaneous events (the same notion is repeated in Revelation with John's book, which is sealed with seven seals) so the very act of opening the book (sealed until the end of time) suggests that one has already initiated the apocalyptic event. Urizen's preoccupation with, and clinging to, his books – as a typical trait of his character – has been previously pointed out but it is only now – complemented with the above argument – that the Szondian parallel attains its full significance: the constant mention of the books and Urizen's obsessive adherence to them not only makes him a perfect example of the *Category of Purism, Moralism and Atonement* – hence a familiar character – , but more importantly, it seems to point to, and emphasize, Urizen's progressive role in the poem.[176]

We can conclude that in *The Four Zoas* the ultimate aesthetic state is associated with Urthona *as well as* Urizen, both being indispensable and complementary to each other, as their names, *dark* Urthona and the Prince of *Light* subtly imply. The very same notion is expressed by the senses that are attributed to them, Urizen being the eyes (eye = I?!) and Urthona corresponding to the ear. Of old there has been pungent debate as to the primacy of one over the other.[177] Ear has had a privileged place because it is known to be the last functioning sense of a dying man and also, in pagan and Christian iconography, ear has often been substituted for the female reproductive organ through which new life can be conceived, metaphorical of new birth and purification. As opposed to the supremacy of the ear, Augustine proposed that the most important of all the senses is the eyes, as it is with the help of visual perception (closely connected to the heart) that one can get closest to God. The only way of reconciling these two opinions is to accept both as inevitable and complementary as propounded by Paul in his first epistle to the Corinthians (12:12–18):

> For as the body is one, and hath many members, and all the members of that one body, being many, are one body: so also *is* Christ. . . .
> For the body is not one member, but many. . . .
> And if the ear shall say, Because I am not the eye, I am not of the body; is it therefore not of the body?
> If the whole body *were* an eye, where *were* the hearing? If the whole *were* hearing, where *were* the smelling? . . .
> But now hath God set the members every one of them in the body, as it hath pleased him.

For the divination of Man, then, a synaesthetic union of eye and ear (the cooperation of Urizen and Urthona) is inevitable; we must hear the word and see the light, as in John 1:14: "And the Word was made flesh, and dwelt among us, and we beheld his glory".

We can conclude that the assertion that Urizen has an underlyingly redemptive role in *The Four Zoas* and that in the poem Reason is just as highly esteemed as Imagination, is substantiated both textually and intertextually.

---

[176] W. J. Mitchell also makes mention of Urizen's association with the book, but his point of departure is substantially different: "In the context of Romantic textual ideology, the book is the symbol of modern rationalistic writing and the cultural economy of mechanical reproduction, while the scroll is the emblem of ancient revealed wisdom, imagination, and the cultural economy of hand-crafted, individually expressive artifacts. . . . The book represents writing as *law*: it is usually associated with patriarchal figures like Urizen and Jehovah. . . . The scroll represents writing as *prophecy*: it is associated with youthful figures of energy, imagination, and rebellion" (*Visible* 137).

[177] My understanding of the role attributed to eye and ear has been informed by Fabiny 39–52.

Finally, one important question needs to be raised. Even though Urizen brings about Albion's redemption, we are constantly reminded "That not of his own power he bore the human form erect / Nor of his own will gave his Laws in times of Everlasting" (VIII, 107:458–459).

A number of Blake scholars have tried to find a satisfactory answer to the puzzling question: Who (or what power) ordains and supervises the events in the universe of the four Zoas?

While Harold Bloom finds that Blake's myth leaves "a saving remnant of Eternity quite unaccountable" (*Blake's* 230), David Punter asserts that it is history that destines every action in the poem. Urizen "does not have true *agency*, his role is dictated to him by an everpresent historical process, and it is this process which gives *The Four Zoas* its unity, beneath the level of fluctuating character relations. Urizen, Tharmas, Los are the prey of history, of a continual dialectic of division and regeneration which is the true agent of the poem" (*Blake, Hegel* 173–174).

A much less deterministic hypothesis is Patricia Cramer's, who postulates that the divine mover is the psyche's self-regulating powers. "The self-balancing tendency arises out of a pre-existent invisible entelechy that continually seeks the reestablishment of unity and harmony among the differentiated parts of the fallen psyche. . . . Blake frequently equates entelechy or soul with 'eternity' – an *a priori* unity of creative contraries" (522).

Although all these aforementioned assumptions contain a seed of truth, the most – textually – justifiable claim is put forth by P. M. S. Dawson. He sees the Council of God as the extrahuman providential reality which oversees the characters from the background.

[Blake] never doubted that man as he existed in the world was fallen, and that any attempt to reverse that fall depended on understanding it – which implied, on justifying it. The trajectory from paradise lost to paradise regained passes through some notion of the fall as *felix culpa*. As a corollary, the whole process is seen as under the control of superintending providence, conceived as extrahuman. Both fall and redemption are stages in a divine plan, which is carried out by human agents of course, but agents who are in necessary ignorance of the nature of what they are doing.[178] Despite Blake's insistent attempts to identify God with humanity, one always arrives back at the sense that human redemption depends on the action of a saviour outside man. (134)

It is important to note that the Council of God is not depicted as forcing Urizen to realize their plans – such an externally imposed solution would be unthinkable – but, in most cases,

---

[178] It is arguable whether or not Urizen is always ignorant of what he has been assigned to do. *The Song of Los* starts with the following prologue:
I will sing you a song of Los. the Eternal Prophet:
He sung it to four harps at the tables of Eternity.
     In heart-formed Africa.
Urizen faded! Ariston shudderd!
     And thus the Song began
Los, the prophet, is describing the future at whose perspective Urizen is terrified and astonished. Critics usually agree that Urizen here is dismayed because the birth of Orc is foretold. But after carefully re-reading the text we may come to a different conclusion. Los is singing his song to "four harps" – perchance to the four Zoas – at the tables of *Eternity*. The Urizen, sitting at the tables of Eternity is the *still unfallen Urizen* – an indubitably positive character – who has nothing to be afraid of Orc. The reason he fades, we may surmise, is that he is let foresee what shall become of him later, what pains the regeneration of Albion really involves. This same realization and fear intermittently appear in *The Four Zoas* as well.

they seem to act in accord with Urizen's own intentions: "And now he came into the Abhorred world of Dark Urthona / By Providence Divine conducted not bent from his own will / Lest death Eternal should be the result for the Will cannot be violated" (VI, 74:280–282). This cooperation is made possible by Urizen's (paroxysmal-epileptiform) character, as in the Cain-phase he pushes the events further into the abyss of experience (hence ever closer to Apocalypse), while in the Moses-stage he is a perfect instrument of the Divine Will.

To sum up Urizen's significance in *The Four Zoas* we can confer that the apparently arbitrarily destructive force he represents carries in it the promise of regeneration for Albion. In the tribulations of the nine nights – through Urizen's prime agency – the Ancient Man becomes a hero, whose status is comparable to the deathless gods.[179] "The gods, though imaged with bodies and bodily appetites, transcend biology, but the hero achieves transcendence only by fulfilling his biological destiny. The gods are immortal, but the hero is *immortalised*" (Austin 111). This symbolic immortality, which Albion attains, is the state of "experiential transcendence", referred to in the second chapter. Besides the extraordinary psychic unity and perceptual intensity, in this state there also occurs a process of symbolic reordering (Lifton 277). The individual, after achieving experiential transcendence, is different from his previous self. The course of symbolic reordering is discernible in Albion too; whereby from Chrestos he becomes Christos:

> The terms Christ and Christians, spelt originally Chrest and Chrestians, were borrowed from the Temple vocabulary of Pagans. Chrestos meant in that vocabulary a disciple on probation, a candidate for hierophantship. When he had attained to this through initiation, long trials and suffering, and had been '*anointed*' . . . his name was changed into *Christos*, the purified, in esoteric or mystery language. In mystic symbology, indeed Christés, or Christos meant that the 'Way' the *Path*, was already trodden and the goal reached; when the fruits of the arduous labour uniting the personality of evanescent clay with the indestructible Individuality, transformed it thereby the immortal EGO.
>
> At the end of the way stands the Chrestes, the Purifier, and the union once accomplished, the Chrestos, the 'man of sorrow', became Christos himself." (Blavatsky 77–78)

What is the birth of *Christos* – the divine Albion in his highest ontological state – on the level of the individual, is the advent of the age of felicity in the universe. The final state of beatitude that is attained here seems to echo Joachim of Flora's third *status*, *ordo monachorum*, a blissful state of *renovatio* preceded by the abomination of desolation (Reeves 402). The Joachimist idea that the coming Age of the Spirit is to be preceded by a terrible chastisement, the instrument of which is an evil agent of divine purpose has informed many a famous and influential tractates from the XIIth century onwards. *The Four Zoas* takes up the notion of the juxtaposition of great evil and great good for *renovatio mundi* and in Urizen's paroxysmal character – in his oscillating facets, which we termed the Urizen-cycle – the medieval idea that the "agents both of *tribulatio* and of *renovatio* are imperial and, indeed . . . the line between the evil oppressor and the just chastiser is not very clear-cut" (Reeves 314) finds an eloquent expression.

---

[179] At the beginning of the poem Albion is not yet God, as Frye so aptly notes: "The identity of God and Man is qualified by the presence in man of the tendency to deny God by self-restriction. Thus, though God is the perfection of man, man is not wholly God; otherwise there would be no point in bringing in the idea of God at all" (*Fearful* 31).

CHAPTER VI

EPILOGUE

I would define Romanticism as chiefly a project of pioneering introspection, aimed at discovering the sources of visionary power, so that each poet could write his or her own mythology, scripture, or testament. Romanticism is intensified introspective individualism, with mythopoeic intent, and Romantic enthusiasms tend to contribute to this project of making one's own interiorized myth, with the help of unexpected, unusual traditionary sources. . . . The greatest Romantic poems are those in which the poet has engaged in such an ambitious and diversified search for the roots of his own imaginative being that the result constitutes a "criticism of life" from the perspective of an intense and cultivated inwardness.

Martin Bidney

"Is there a word for someone who ignores or abridges everyday commonly accepted reality for the sake of a belief? Indeed there is: such a person is a fanatic. . . . We find in *Paradise Lost* a poet bravely, grandly attempting to be fanatical but undermined by his reasonableness on almost every page. Then *are* there any fanatical poets in English. There is Shelley ... But there is a firmer ground in another quarter: William Blake" (Moore 180–181).

The platform from which we investigated the "fanatical" ideas of Blake was *The Four Zoas*, a most recalcitrant work of the time.

The question pertains: What makes *The Four Zoas* "as mad as the effort to play croquet in Wonderland with living mallets and balls" (Erdman, *Prophet* 294) and, correspondingly what makes Blake "one of the great pugilists of intellectual history" (Eaves, *William Blake's* 6).

We have found that the central trope of the poem is the prevalent Romantic idea of life as a journey, the Christian *peregrinatio,* as elucidated by radical Inner Light hermeneutics, assimilating Neoplatonic ideas. In the focus of the poem is the search for the lost unity, but Blake dissents from Plotinos in his essentially teleological approach to history, inasmuch as the movement from the One to the many is depicted as a justifiable evil, an indispensable step in the ascention towards wholeness and perfection – ideas that conjoin the major emphases of contemporary German philosophy. The conceptual framework of the poem, then, cannot be considered to account for the interpretative cruxes.

The question of how the framework is filled in now arises.

The romantic mind assumes the task of perceiving and expressing the all, and even more relating to it. Ways of managing this task abound. Metaphors of marriage, the harmonizing of faculties and emotions, the rhetorical figure of synaesthesia, the new aesthetic emphasis on the sublime, . . . states of possession and psychic pathology, androgyny, and even incest: all these can be recognized as part of the search for forms that can survive at the juncture of personal integrity and structural wholeness. (Cooke, 438)

All these literary devices Blake deployed ... and much more. The most immediate reason for the genuine difficulty of the poem appears to be found in Blake's complete abandonment of conventional narrative forms – also called Newtonian narrative – , which presupposes behind the text a single, unified world, to be substituted by a narrative field of open present and past, which can be altered by perspective transformations or prequels.

It is inevitable that, in assaulting his reader so aggressively with presuppositions and techniques that fundamentally conflict with Newtonian narrative and thus with habitual thought processes and conventional narrative procedures, Blake risked losing most of the audience he intended for the poem. . . . Moreover, in order to square his philosophical principles with the narrative strategies they demand – which include a continual teaching of subversive narrative rules and a subsequent testing of the reader's imaginative judgement in the terms of those rules, a continual laying of traps to ensnare, especially, the Newtonian reader – he risked, almost invited, a total misunderstanding of the poem even by those readers more sympathetic to his program. (Ault, *Re-Visioning* 109)

The sustained suspense of the narrative through perspective transformation/prequels is made possible by the characters that inhabit the epic; the Zoas, Blake's most original inventions.

Besides the taxing narrative, the Zoas' polysemantic reference presents special problems. We have approached these figures from an underlyingly psychological point of view, a reading justified by several textual evidences which reveal them as components of the human psyche. In a piece of literature "psychological truth is an artistic value only if it enhances coherence and complexity – if, in short, it is art" (Wellek and Warren 93).

In *The Four Zoas* the above precept is eloquently fulfilled, and a close exploration of the characters has disclosed that certain tenets of critical consensus concerning these mental faculties are insufficient, and indeed account for much of the conceptual polemics and the corresponding aversion in connection with the poem.

Most conspicuously our investigations have shown that the preconceived ideas based on the readings of the minor prophecies constitute the main stumbling block and that Blake's poetry cannot be considered as made up of monolithic ideas – Romantic *per se* – but rather, it is to be seen as gradually changing. This assumption is best supported by the emergence of a fourfold system of correlations, embodied in the Zoas. The significant role of Tharmas/senses in the process of ontological awakening, the Urizen-cycle in the place of the subsequent – essentially negative – portrayal of the Zoa of reason, closely connected with the ambivalent depiction of Luvah/emotions as well as the relatively minor, and pronouncedly changed role of Los/imagination all indicate that in *The Four Zoas* – compared to *The Book of Urizen* – we are to witness considerable conceptual changes; among the Romantic ideas previously rejected Enlightenment values are adopted as essential to the achievement of perfection, the divinity of Albion. Tharmas and Urizen are accepted as integral part of the human, faithful to the spirit of St. Paul:

But now are they many members, yet but one body.
And the eye cannot say unto the hand, I have no need of thee: nor again the head to the feet, I have no need of you.
Nay, much more those members of the body, which seem to be more feeble, are necessary:
And those members of the body, which we think to be less honourable, upon these

we bestow more abundant honour; and our uncomely parts have more abundant comeliness.

For our comely parts have no need: but God hath tempered the body together, having given more abundant honour to that part which lacked:

There should be no schism in the body; but that the members should have the same care one for another.

And whether one member suffer, all the members suffer with it; or one member be honoured, all the members rejoice with it. (Corinthians I, 12:20–26)

As we have found that the four Zoas represent the four main character types, thus their quaternity embody the whole of mankind, the acceptance of all of them as of equal merit in *The Four Zoas* can be seen as a poetic rendering of Blake's essential Humanity.

APPENDIX

APPENDIX I

ALAN MILLER'S PERSONALITY TYPES

	Analytical Scientist (Reductionist)	Conceptual Theorist (Schematist)	Conceptual Humanist (Romantic)	Particular-Humanist (Gnostic)
Nature of Science	Occupies a privileged and preferred position: clearly separable from other fields and clear lines of demarcation between disciplines; value-free, disinterested, apolitical	Occupies a privileged and preferred position; not clearly separable from other fields, all disciplines depend on one another; value-free and apolitical	Does *not* occupy a privileged and preferred position; not clearly separable from other fields and all disciplines depend on one another; science is *not* value-free, it is political	Does *not* occupy a privileged and preferred position; may be subordinate to poetry, art, literature, music, and mysticism as older "superior" ways of knowing; science is political
Nature of Scientific knowledge	Impersonal. value-free, disinterested; precise, reliable, accurate, valid, reductionistic and realistic, unambiguous; apolitical	Impersonal, value-free, disinterested; imaginative, holistic, ambiguous, uncertain; apolitical	Personal value-based; imaginative, holistic, uncertain and multiple causation; political and concerned with humanity	Personal, value-based; acausal, non-rational; partisan, political; sometimes action-oriented
Basis of Truth	Consensus, agreement, reliability, external validity, rigor, controlled nature of inquiry	Conflict between antithetical imaginative theories; comprehensive, integrative theory building	Conflict between objective and subjective knowledge; between the knower and the known	Intense personal knowledge and experience
Aims of Science	Precise, unambiguous theoretical and empirical knowledge	To construct the broadest possible conceptual schemes	To promote human development on the widest possible scale	To help people know themselves and to achieve self-determination
Role of Science	Disinterested, unbiased, impersonal, sceptical experts and specialists	Disinterested, unbiased, impersonal, imaginative, speculative generalists	Personally involved, admitting of biases, imaginative, speculative generalists	Personally involved, biased, imaginative, poetical interpreters of the particular

APPENDIX II

THE DRIVE SYSTEM OF THE EXPERIMENTAL DIAGNOSTICS OF DRIVES

Drive tendencies	Drive factors	Drive vectors
1. Tendency to personal sensual affection. 2. Tendency to collective humanitarian kindness.	I. Femininity maternalism h factor	I. S Vector Sexual Drive
3. Tendency to sadism; aggression, activity. 4. Tendency to civilization, generosity, humility, sacrifice, passivity, masochism.	II. Masculinity s factor III. Ethics,	
5. Tendency to evil, accumulation of rage, hatred anger, vengeance, injustice, intolerance, "Cain". 6. Tendency to good, collective justice, tolerance, kindness, mercy, devotion, "Abel".	Cain and Abel trends e factor	II. P vector ethics drive
7. Tendency to shameless self-exhibiton. 8. Tendency to collective shamefacedness.	IV. Need or attention exhibitionism hy factor	emotional discharge paraoxysmal drive
9. Tendency to autism, egotism, egocentricity, narcissism, introjction. 10. Tendency to adjustment to the collective, repression.	V. Ego constriction, ego systole, adjustive, matrcialistic ego, k factor	III. Sch vector ego drive
11. Tendency to ego-expansion, to seize power, blame others (projection). 12. Tendency to spread humanitarian ideals, spirtual values.	VI. Ego expanson, ego diastole, spiritual go, p factor	
13. Tendency to acquisition to the disadvantage of others, search for new ojects disloyalty. 14. Tendency to self-denial for the sake of all people, loyalty, anality.	VII. Need to appropiate, searching, d factor	IV. C vector contact drive
15. Tendency to cling to the old object (thing person); orality, hedonism. 16. Tendency to sepaate, to loneliness.	VIII. Need to cling dependently, m factor	

APPENDIX III

COMPUTER ANALYSIS OF "THE FOUR ZOAS"

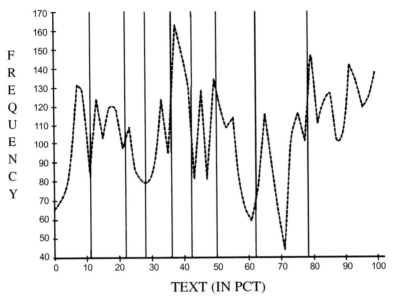

1. The positioning of the Nights along an axis representing the entire text

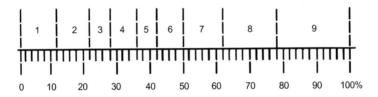

2. Distribution of image density across the text of "The Four Zoas"

127

BIBLIOGRAPHY

Abrahams, C. A. *William Blake's Fourfold Man*. Bonn: Bouvier Verlag Herbert Grundmann, 1978.

Abrams, M. H. *Natural Supernaturalism: Tradition and Revolution in Romantic Literature*. New York, London: Norton, 1971.

Ackland, Michael. "The Embattled Sexes: Blake's Dept to Wollstonecraft in *The Four Zoas*." *Blake: An Illustrated Quarterly* 16, no. 3 (Winter 1982–83): 172–183.

Aers, David. "The Representations of Revolution: From *The French Revolution* to *The Four Zoas*." Punter, *William Blake* 165–187.

Albright, Daniel. *The Myth against Myth: A Study of Yeats's Imagination in Old Age*. London: Oxford University Press, 1972.

Altizer, Thomas J. J. *The New Apocalypse: The Radical Christian Vision of William Blake*. East Lansing: Michigan, 1967.

History as Apocalypse. Albany: State University of New York Press, 1985.

Aronoff, D., et al. *Psychology Today*. Del Mar: CRM Books, 1970.

Ault, Donald. "Incommensurability and Interconnection in Blake's Anti-Newtonian Text." *Studies in Romanticism* 16, no.3 (Summer 1977): 277–305.

Narrative Unbound: Re-visioning William Blake's "The Four Zoas". Barrytown, New York: Station Hill Press, 1987.

"Blake's De-Formation of Neo-Aristotelianism." Miller–Bracher–Ault 111–139.

"Re-Visioning *The Four Zoas*." Hilton and Vogler 105–140.

Austin, Norman. *Meaning and Being in Myth*. University Park and London: Pennsylvania State University Press, 1990.

Bachelard, Gaston. *La psychanalyse du feu*. Paris: Gallimard, 1949.

Ba-Han, Maung. *Blake: His Mysticism*. Bordeaux, 1924.

Beer, John. *Blake's Visionary Universe*. New York: Manchester University Press, 1969.

Behrendt, Steven C. "'The Consequence of High Powers': Blake, Shelley and Prophecy's Dimension." *Papers on Language and Literature* 22, no. 3 (1986): 254–275.

Bentley, G.E., Jr., ed. *Vala or The Four Zoas*. Oxford: Clarendon Press, 1963.

Blake Records. Oxford: Clarendon Press, 1969.

William Blake's Writings. 2 vols. Oxford: Clarendon Press, 1978.

Bentley, G. E., Jr., and Martin K. Nurmi. *A Blake Bibliography: Annotated Lists of Works, Studies and Blakeana*. Minneapolis, 1964.

Bereczkei, Tamás. "Biológiai evolúció, genotropizmus, pszichopatológia: A Szondi-elmélet újraértelmezése."[Biological Evolution, Genotropism and Psychopathology: A Reinterpretation of Szondi's theory]. *Thalassza* 4, no.1 (1993): 150–172.

Berger, Paul. *William Blake: Poet and Mystic*. Trans. D. H. Conner. London, 1914.

Bidlake, Steven. "Blake, the Sacred, and the French Revolution: 18th-Century Ideology and the Problem of Violence." *European Romantic Review* 3, no.1 (Summer 1992): 1–20.

Bidney, Martin. *Blake and Goethe: Psychology, Ontology, Imagination*. Columbia: University of Missouri Press, 1988.

Bindman, David. *Blake as an Artist*. Oxford: Phaidon, 1977.

Birenbaum, Harvey. *Myth and Mind*. Boston: University Press of America, 1988.

Blake, William. *The Complete Poetry and Prose of William Blake*. Ed. David V. Erdman, commentary by Harold Bloom. Newly revised ed. Berkeley and Los Angeles: University of California Press, 1982.

Blavatsky, H. P. *The Theosophical Glossary*. Krotona: Theosophical Publishing House, 1918.

Bloom, Harold. *The Visionary Company: A Reading of English Romantic Poetry*. London: Faber and Faber, 1961.

   Blake's Apocalypse: A Study in Poetic Argument. Ithaca, New York: Cornell University Press, 1970.

Blunt, Anthony. "Blake's Glad Day." *Journal of Wartburg & Courtauld Institute* 2 (1938).

Borges, Jorge L. *A titkos csoda*. [The Secret Miracle] Budapest: Európa, 1986.

Botond Ágnes. *Pszichohistória – avagy a lélek történetiségének tudománya*. [Psychohistory: The Science of the History of the Mind] Budapest: Tankönyvkiadó, 1991.

Bronowsky, Jacob. *William Blake: A Man Without a Mask*. London, 1943.

Butlin, Martin. *The Paintings and Drawings of William Blake*. 2 vols. New Haven and London: Yale University Press, 1981.

Butterworth, A. M. *Blake, Mystic*. Liverpool and London, 1911.

Camus, Albert. *Théâtre, récits, nouvelles*. Paris: Gallimard, 1991. (Bibliothéque de la Pléiade)

Casier, Esther. "William Blake: A Study in Religious Sublimation." *Catholic World* (March 1946): 518–525.

Clark, Lorraine. *Blake, Kierkegaard, and the Spectre of Dialectic*. Cambridge: Cambridge University Press, 1991.

Cooke, Michael J. "Romanticism and the Paradox of Wholeness." *Studies in Romanticism* 23, no. 4 (Winter 1984): 435–455.

Cooper, Andrew M. *Doubt and Identity in Romantic Poetry*. New Haven and London: Yale University Press, 1988.

Cramer, Patricia. "The Role of Ahania's Lament in Blake's *Book of Ahania*: A Psychoanalytic Study." *Journal of English and German Philology* 83, no. 4 (1984): 522–533.

Damon, S. Foster. *William Blake: His Philosophy and Symbols*. Boston: Houghton Mifflin Company, 1924.

   Blake's Job: William Blake's Illustrations of the Book of Job. Providence: Brown University Press, 1966.

   A Blake Dictionary: The Ideas and Symbols of William Blake. University Press of New England, 1988.

Dawson, P. M. S. "Blake and Providence: The Theodicy of *The Four Zoas*." *Blake: An Illustrated Quarterly* 20, no.4 (Spring 1987): 134–144.

De Luca, Vincent A. "Blake and Burke in Astonishment!" *Blake: An Illustrated Quarterly* 23, no. 2 (Fall 1989): 100–104.

Deri, Susan. *Introduction to the Szondi Test: Theory and Practice*. New York: Grune and Stratton, 1949.

Eaves, Morris. "Inside the Blake Industry: Past, Present and Future." *Studies in Romanticism* 21, no. 3 (Fall 1982): 389–391.

   William Blake's Theory of Art. Princeton: Princeton University Press, 1982.

Edwards, Gavin. "Repeating the Same Dull Round." Punter, *William Blake* 108–122.

Egri Péter. *Literature, Painting and Music*. Budapest: Akadémiai, 1988.

Eliade, Mircea. *Az örök visszatérés mítosza avagy a mindenség és a történelem*. [The Myth of Eternal Return] Budapest: Európa, 1993.

Eliot, Thomas S. *The Sacred Wood: Essays on Poetry and Criticism*. London: Methuen, 1928.

Erdman, David V. *Prophet Against Empire*. Princeton: Princeton University Press, 1954.

   ed. *A Concordance to the Writings of William Blake*. 2 vols. Ithaca: Cornell University Press, 1967.

Essick, Robert N. *William Blake, Printmaker.* Princeton: Princeton University Press, 1980.

Fabinyi, Tibor. "A szem és a fül: Látás és hallás hermeneutikai konfliktusa." [Eyes and Ears: The Hermeneutical Conflict of Vision and Hearing] *Pannonhalmi Szemle* 3, no.1 (1995): 39–52.

Finch, G. J. "Blake and Civilization." *English* 40, no.168 (Autumn 1991): 200–208.

Fogel, Aaron. "Pictures of Speech: On Blake's Poetic." *Studies in Romanticism* 21, no. 2 (Summer 1982): 217–242.

Frye, Northrop. *Fearful Symmetry: A Study of William Blake.* Princeton: Princeton University Press, 1947.

   The Great Code: The Bible and Literature. London: Routledge & Kegan Paul, 1982.

   "Blake's Treatment of the Archetype." Johnson and Grant 510–525.

Fuller, David. *Blake's Heroic Argument.* London, New York, Sydney: Croom Helm, 1988.

Gallant, Christine. *Blake and the Assimilation of Chaos.* Princeton: Princeton University Press, 1978.

George, Diane Hume. *Blake and Freud.* Ithaca: Cornell University Press, 1980.

Gilchrist, Alexander. *Life of William Blake: Pictor Ignotus.* London: Macmillan, 1863.

Glausser, Wayne. "The Gates of Memory in Night VIIa of *The Four Zoas.*" *Blake: An Illustrated Quarterly* 18, no.4 (Spring 1985): 196–204.

Goldsmith, Steven. *Unbuilding Jerusalem: Apocalypse and Romantic Representation.* Ithaca and London: Cornell University Press, 1993.

Gross, David. "'Mind-Forg'd Manacles': Hegemony and Counterhegemony in Blake." *Eighteenth Century* 27, no.1 (1986): 3–25.

Groves, David. "Blake, Thomas Boston and the Fourfold Vision." *Blake: An Illustrated Quarterly* 19, no.4 (Spring 1986): 146.

Hagstrum, Jean A. "Babylon Revisited, or the Story of Luvah and Vala." Punter, *William Blake* 36–53.

Haigney, Catherine. "Vala's Garden in Night the Ninth: Paradise Regained or Women Bound?" *Blake: An Illustrated Quarterly* 20, no.4 (Spring 1984): 116–125.

Haigwood, Laura. "Blake's *Visions of the Daughters of Albion:* Revising an Interpretive Tradition." Punter, *William Blake* 94–107.

Hall, Jason Y. "Gall's Phrenology: A Romantic Psychology." *Studies in Romanticism* 16, no. 3 (Summer 1977): 305–317.

Hamblen, E. S. *On the Minor Prophecies of William Blake.* New York, 1968.

Hárs, György P. "Nyelv, alkímia és pszichoanalízis." [Language, alchemy and psyhoanalysis] *Thalassza* 4, no.1 (1993): 70–80.

Hillman, James. *Healing Fiction.* Station Hill, 1983.

Hilton, Nelson. "Becoming Prolific Being Devoured." *Studies in Romanticism* 21, no.3 (Fall 1982): 417–425.

   Literal Imagination: Blake's Vision of Words. Berkeley, Los Angeles and London: University of California Press, 1983.

   "Some Sexual Connotations." *Blake: An Illustrated Quarterly* 16, no. 3 (Winter 1982–83): 166–171.

   "Blake in the Chains of Being." Punter, *William Blake* 71–93.

Hilton, Nelson, and Thomas A. Vogler, eds. *Unnam'd Forms: Blake and Textuality.* Berkeley, Los Angeles and London: University of California Press, 1986.

Hume, Robert D. "The Development of Blake's Psychology: The Quest for an Understanding of Man's Position in the World." *Revue Des Langues Vivantes* 35, no. 3 (1969): 240–258.

Iazumi, Yoko. "Brotherhood in Blake: Psychology and Poetics." *DAI* 46 (1985): 11A. Yale University

Ide, Nancy M. "Image Patterns and the Structure of William Blake's *The Four Zoas.*" *Blake: An Illustrated Quarterly* 20, no. 4 (Spring 1987): 125–134.

"Identifying Semantic Patterns: Time Series and Fourier Analysis." *Revue Informatique et Statistique dans les Sciences humanies* 24, nos.1–4 (1988): 193–221.

"A Statistical Measure of Theme and Structure." *Computers and the Humanities* 23, nos. 4–5 (Aug-Oct. 1989): 277–285.

Jamain, Alain. "A sorsanalízis helye a freudizmusban." (The use of Szondi Test in the Freudianism) *Pszichológia* 14, no. 2 (1994): 181–184.

James, David E. "Angels out of the Sun: Art, Religion and Politics in Blake's *America.*" Punter, *William Blake* 54–70.

"Joachim of Flora." *The Oxford Dictionary of the Christian Church.* 1958 ed.

Johnson, Mary Lynn, and John E.Grant, eds. *Blake's Poetry and Designs.* New York, London: Norton, 1979.

Jung, Carl Gustav. *Emlékek, álmok, gondolatok.* [Memoirs, Dreams, Reflections] Budapest: Európa, 1987.

    A lélektani típusok általános leírása. [Personality Types] Budapest: Európa, 1988.

    Analitikus pszichológia. [Analytical Psychology] Budapest: Göncöl, 1991.

    Válasz Jób könyvére. [Answer to Job] Budapest: Akadémiai, 1992.

Kermode, F., and J. Hollander, eds. *The Oxford Anthology of English Literature.* Oxford: Oxford University Press, 1985.

Kittel, Harold A. "*The Book of Urizen* and *An Essay Concerning Human Understanding.*" Phillips 111–144.

Kon, I. Sz. *Énünk nyomában: A személyiség és én-tudata.* [*V poiskah seba*] Budapest: Kossuth, 1989.

Lee, Judith. "Scornful Beauty: A Note on Blake and Ariosto." *English Language Notes* 23, no. 4 (1986): 36–38.

Lifton, Robert J. "The Sense of Immortality: On Death and the Continuity of Life." Lifton and Olson 271–288.

Lifton, Robert J., and Eric Olson, eds. *Explorations is Psychohistory.* New York: Simon and Schuster, 1974.

Lindsay, Jack. *William Blake: His Life and Work.* New York: George Braziller, 1979.

Lukács, Dénes. *A Szondi-teszt.* [The Szondi Test] Budapest: Tankönyvkiadó, 1991.

    Szondi: Az ösztönprofiltól az elméletig. (From Drive Scheme to Theory) Budapest: Animula, 1996.

Mann, Paul. "The Final State of *The Four Zoas.*" *Blake: An Illustrated Quarterly* 18, no.4 (Spring 1985): 204–216.

    "*The Book of Urizen* and the Horizon of the Book." Hilton and Vogler 49–68.

McGann, Jerome J. "The Idea of an Indeterminate Text: Blake's Bible of Hell and Dr. Alexander Geddes." *Studies in Romanticism* 25, no. 3 (1986): 303–325.

Mee, Jon. *Dangerous Enthusiasm: William Blake and the Culture of Radicalism in the 1790s.* Oxford: Clarendon Press, 1992

Mellor, Anne K. "Blake's Portrayal of Women." *Blake: An Illustrated Quarterly* 16, no. 3 (Winter 1982–83): 148–155.

Miller, Alan. *Personality Types: A Modern Synthesis.* University of Calgary Press, 1991.

Miller, D., M. Bracher, and D. Ault, eds. *Blake and the Argument of Method.* Durham and London: Duke University Press, 1987.

Mitchell, W. J. T. "Style as Epistemology: Blake and the Movement toward Abstraction in Romantic Art." *Studies in Romanticism* 16, no.2 (Spring 1977): 145–165.

    "Dangerous Blake." *Studies in Romanticism* 21, no.3 (Fall 1982): 410–416.

    "Visible Language: Blake's Wond'rous Art of Writing." Punter, *William Blake* 123–148.

Moore, Richard. "Fanatical Poets and Reasonable Poets." *Stanford Literature Review* 4, no. 2 (Fall 1987): 175–193.

Morton, A. L. *The Everlasting Gospel: A Study in the Sources of William Blake*. London: Lawrence and Wishart, 1958.

Noszlopi, László. *Sorselemzés és kísérleti ösztöndiagnosztika: A Szondi-féle ösztönlélektan teljes ismertetése*. [Fate Analysis and Experimental Diagnostics of Drives: A Complete Guide to Szondi's Theory of Drives] Budapest: Akadémiai, 1989.

Ogilvy, James. *Many Dimensional Man: Decentralizing Self, Society, and the Sacred*. New York: Oxford University Press, 1977.

Ostriker, Alicia. "Desire Gratified and Ungratified: William Blake and Sexuality." *Blake: An Illustrated Quarterly* 16, no. 3 (Winter 1982–83): 156–165.

Otto, Peter. "Final States, Finished Forms, and *The Four Zoas*." *Blake: An Illustrated Quarterly* 20, no.4 (Spring 1987): 144–146.

Patai József. *A Biblia képekben. Klasszikus és modern mesterek remekművei*. [The Bible in Pictures: Classic and Modern Masterpieces] Budapest, 1924.

Péter, Ágnes. *Roppant szivárvány: A romantikus látásmódról*. (An Awful Rainbow) Budapest: Nemzeti Tankönyvkiadó, 1996.

Peterfreund, Stuart. "The Din of the City in Blake's Prophetic Books." *ELH* 64, no.1 (Spring 1997): 99–130.

Phillips, Michael, ed. *Interpreting Blake*. Cambridge: Cambridge University Press, 1978.

Pierce, John B. "The Shifting Characterization of Tharmas and Enion in Pages 3–7 of Blake's *Vala or The Four Zoas*." *Blake: An Illustrated Quarterly* 22, no. 3 (Winter 1988–89): 93–102.

Pléh Csaba. *Pszichológiatörténet: A modern pszichológia kialakulása*. [A History of Psychology: The Development of Modern Psychology] Budapest: Gondolat, 1992.

Pomper, Philip. *The Structure of Mind in History: Five Major Figures in Psychohistory*. New York: Columbia University Press, 1985.

Pulley, N. "Note on Freud and Blake." *International Journal of Psycho Analysis* 6 (1925) 51–52.

Punter, David. *Blake, Hegel and Dialectic*. Amsterdam: Rodopi, 1982.

——— "Blake, Trauma and the Female." *New Literary History* 15, no.3 (1984): 475–491.

——— ed. *William Blake*. London: Macmillan, 1996.

Quasha, George. "Orc as a Fiery Paradigm of Poetic Torsion." Punter, *William Blake* 16–35.

Raine, Kathleen. *Blake and Tradition*. 2 vols. Bollingen Series, no. 35, vol. 11. Princeton: Princeton University Press, 1968.

——— *Golgonooza, City of Imagination: Last Studies in William Blake*. Ipswich: Golgonooza Press, 1991.

Rajan, Tilottama. *The Form of the Unfinished: English Poetics from Spenser to Pound*. Princeton: Princeton University Press, 1985.

Reeves, Marjorie. *The Influence of Prophecy in the Later Middle Ages: A Study in Joachimism*. Oxford: Clarendon Press, 1969.

Rosso, G.A. "History and Apocalypse in Blake's *The Four Zoas*: The Final Nights." Rosso and Watkins 173–189.

Rosso, G. A., and D. P. Watkins, eds. *Spirits of Fire: English Romantic Writers and Contemporary Historical Methods*. London and Toronto: Associated University Presses, 1990.

Rotenberg, Bettina. "Blake's Contraries: A Poetics of Visionary Perception." *European Romantic Review* 2, no.1 (Summer 1991): 81–99.

Saintsbury, George. *A History of Criticism and Literary Taste in Europe*. 3 vols. Edinburgh and London: William Blackwood & Sons, 1904.

Sampson, J., ed. *The Poetical Works of William Blake*. Oxford: Clarendon Press, 1905.

Santarcangeli, Paolo. "*Pokolra kell annak menni ...:": Költők pokoljárása*. [Nekyia] Trans. Márta Farkas, and Judit Kepes. Budapest: Gondolat, 1980.

Schorer, Mark. *William Blake: The Politics of Vision*. New York: Henry Holt, 1946.

Schuchard, Marsha K. "Blake's Healing Trio: Magnetism, Medicine and Mania." *Blake: An Illustrated Quarterly* 23, no.1 (Summer 1989): 20–32.

133

Sheel Singh, Charu. *The Chariot of Fire: A Study of William Blake in the Light of Hindu Thought.* Oxford, 1981.

Simpson, David. "Reading Blake and Derrida – Our Caesars neither Praised nor Buried." Punter, *William Blake* 149–164.

Singer, June. *The Unholy Bible: Blake, Jung and the Collective Unconscious.* Boston: Sigo Press, 1986.

Androgyny: The Opposites Within. Boston: Sigo Press, 1989.

Sloss, D. J., and J. P. R.Wallis, eds. *Prophetic Writings.* Oxford, 1926.

Spector, Sheila A. "Hebraic Etymologies of Proper Names in Blake's Myth." *Philological Quarterly* 67, no. 3 (1988): 345–363.

Stempel, Daniel. "Identifying Ahania: Etymology and Iconology in Blake's Allegorical Nomenclature." *Studies in Romanticism* 28, no.1 (1989): 95–119.

Storch, Margaret. "The 'Spectrous Fiend' is Cast Out: Blake's Crisis at Felpham." *Modern Language Quarterly* 44 (1983): 115–135.

Symons, Arthur. *William Blake.* New York, 1907.

Szegedy-Maszák Mihály. *Kubla kán és Pickwick úr: Romantika és realizmus az angol irodalomban.* [Kubla Khan and Mr Pickwick: Romanticism and Realism in English Literature] Budapest: Magvetõ, 1982.

Szenczi Miklós. *William Blake: Versek és Próféciák.* [William Blake: Poems and Prophecies] Budapest: Európa, 1959.

"Blake tanítása a képzeletrõl." [Blake on Imagination] Szenczi, *Tanulmányok* 333–347.

Tanulmányok. [Essays] Budapest: Akadémiai, 1989.

Szerb Antal. *William Blake.* [William Blake] Szeged: Szeged Városi Nyomda és Könyvkiadó RT, 1928.

Szondi, Lipót. *Az ember meghatározása az ösztönök tapasztalati rendszerében: Az ember ösztön-linneusa.* [Defining the Self with the Szondi test] Budapest, 1942.

Az Én kísérleti elemzése. [Experimentelle Triebdiagnostic] (Experimental Diagnostics of the Self) Budapest, 1943.

Módszertan és ösztöntan. [Diagnosis of Drives] Budapest, 1943.

Experimental Diagnostics of Drives. Trans. Gertrude Aull. New York: Grune and Stratton, 1952.

Káin, a Törvényszegõ. Mózes, a Törvényalkotó. [Kain Gestalten des Bösen. Moses. Antwort auf Kain] Trans. Vera Mérei. Budapest: Gondolat, 1987.

Ember és Sors. [Man and Fate] Budapest: Kossuth, 1996.

Szondi, Lipót, Ulrich Moser and M. W. Webb. *The Szondi Test: In Diagnosis, Prognosis and Treatment.* Philadelphia and Montreal: Lippincott, 1958.

Tannenbaum, Leslie. *Biblical Tradition in Blake's Early Prophecies: The Great Code of Art.* Princeton: Princeton University Press, 1982.

Tatham, Frederick. *The Life of Blake.* [c.1832]. First published with Letters, ed. A. G. B. Russell 1906.

Van Meerbeek, Jeanne-Pierre. "Az ösztönsémák Jean Piaget elméletén alapuló pszichogenetikai értelmezése." [The psychogenetical interpretation of schemata of instincts based on Jean Piaget's theory] *Pszichológia* 14, no. 2 (1994): 185–190.

Vargha, András. "A Szondi-teszt faktorainak kísérleti vizsgálata." [An experimental study of the factors of Szondi-test] *Magyar Pszichológiai Szemle* 36 (1979): 498–511.

"Néhány újabb eredmény a Szondi-teszt validitásával kapcsolatban." [Some new results with respect the validation of the Szondi-test] *Pszichológia* 8, no.1 (1988): 3–28.

"Új személyiségskálák a Szondi-teszt képeinek felhasználásával, I: A Szondi-képek információtartalma."[Construction of new personality scales by means of the pictures of the

Szondi Test, I.: The information content of the 48 Szondi-pictures] *Pszichológia* 9, no. 4 (1989): 551–592.

"Új személyiségskálák a Szondi-teszt képeinek felhasználásával, II: Konstrukció és reliabilitásvizsgálat." [II Construction and check of reliability] *Pszichológia* 10, no. 1 (1990): 85–120.

"Új személyiségskálák a Szondi-teszt képeinek felhasználásával, III: Az új skálák pszichológiai jelentésének vizsgálata." [III Validation] *Pszichológia* 10, no. 2 (1990): 209–277.

"Újabb adalékok a Szondi-teszt pszichometriájához." [New data on the psychology of the Szondi Test] *Pszichológia* 14, no.2 (1994): 199–268.

A Szondi-teszt pszichometriája. [The Psychometry of the Szondi Test] Budapest: Universitatis, 1994.

Verma, K. D. "The Woman Figure in Blake and the Idea of Shakti in Indian Thought." *Comparative Literature Studies* 27, no. 3 (1990): 193–211.

Vikár, György. "A Szondi-teszt használata rövid analitikus pszichoterápiában." [The use of Szondi Test in the short analytical psychometry]*Pszichológia* 14, no. 2 (1994): 173–180.

Webster, Brenda S. *Blake's Prophetic Psychology.* London: Macmillan Press, 1983.

"Blake, Woman and Sexuality." Punter, *William Blake* 188–206.

Wellek, René, and Austin Warren. *Theory of Literature.* 3rd ed. New Haven, Conn.: Penguin, 1962.

White, Helen C. *The Mysticism of William Blake.* Madison: University of Wisconsin Press, 1927.

Wilkie, Brian, and Mary Lynn Johnson. *Blake's Four Zoas: The Design of a Dream.* Cambridge, Mass. and London, England: Harvard University Press, 1978.

Wilkie, Brian. "The Romantic Ideal of Unity." *Studies in Literary Imagination* 19, no. 2 (Fall 1986): 5–23.

Woodman, Ross. "Shaman, Poet, and Failed Initiative: Reflections on Romanticism and Jungian Psychology." *Studies in Romanticism* 19, no. 1 (Spring 1980): 51–83.

Youngquist, Paul. *Madness in Blake's Myth.* University Park and London: Pennsylvania State University Press, 1989.

LIST OF ILLUSTRATIONS

LIST OF ABBREVIATIONS

BA	The Book of Ahania
BoL	The Book of Los
BU	The Book of Urizen
DesC	A Descriptive Catalogue of Pictures
ELG	The Everlasting Gospel
FZ	The Four Zoas
J	Jerusalem
M	Milton, a Poem in 2 Books
MHH	The Marriage of Heaven and Hell
SoL	The Song of Los
VLJ	[A Vision of the Last Judgement]